One Flesh

An Intimacy Guide for Married Couples

One
Flesh

*An Intimacy Guide for
Married Couples*

by

Clay McConkie, Ph.D.

ISBN: 1-55517-524-4
v.1

Published by Bonneville Books

Distributed by:
925 North Main, Springville, UT 84663 • 801/489-4084

CFI Publishing and Distribution Since 1986

Cedar Fort, Incorporated
CFI Distribution • CFI Books • Council Press • Bonneville Books

Typeset by Virginia Reeder
Cover design by Adam Ford
Cover design © 2001 by Lyle Mortimer

Printed in the United States of America

Genesis 2:24

"Therefore shall a man leave his father and his mother, and shall cleave unto his wife: and they shall be one flesh."

Author

Clay McConkie is a native of Utah. He is a teacher by occupation, having taught in the Salt Lake City Schools for thirty years. He received a B.A. from Brigham Young University and an M.S. and Ph.D. from the University of Utah. He and his wife reside in Provo, Utah, and are the parents of four children.

To All
Who Are Married
or
Plan to Be

Note on Repetition

In the material that follows, repetition is a significant factor. Since each chapter is written as a separate article, independent from the others, continual reference to certain concepts and ideas will sometimes appear redundant. The advantage of emphasis and reinforcement, however, will hopefully outweigh any disadvantage of the other.

Table of Contents

Preface   xi
The Magic Triangle   1
Think Before You Marry   9
Rules of Marriage   15
The Magic Ring   29
Jed and Nancy   35
Marriage and Chastity   41
An Ounce of Prevention   47
A Matter of Rights   53
Honeymoon Revisited   61
Sexuality and Spirituality   67
The Red Rose and the White   77
To Be One Flesh   87
A Theory of Merging Circles   93
Epilogue   113
Note   117

Poetry   119
Capri   119
Woman at a Grocery Store   121
A Simple Thing   124
Equality   126
A Place by the Sea   128

Preface

A famous English poet once said that beauty is truth, and truth beauty. And then he added, "That is all ye know on earth and all ye need to know." The same principle might apply to the contents of this book. Sexual relations after marriage, *and not before*, can be a beautiful thing, and as they pertain to a marital relationship, the truth concerning them is one of the most important things that a person can know.

Yet obviously there is a problem. Too many marriages, for example, end in separation or divorce, not to mention those that continue to endure year after year despite incompatibility. It might be that two-thirds of today's marriages, in fact, or possibly even more, do not turn out as people would like them to be.

Many have discussed such a problem and have given their opinions as to how it might be corrected. They suggest many different kinds of preventions or cures which theoretically will provide solutions, yet things have not changed, and the number of separations still continues to increase.

The purpose of this book, therefore, is to add one more opinion to what has already been said, a very different one in some ways since it focuses so heavily upon intimacy and sexuality. It includes a series of independent articles directed to all mature age groups and deals mainly with marital sex, its necessity and desirability, and especially the fact that it can be a thing of beauty.

There is also the specific question as to how couples can stay together and avoid separation or divorce. This has always been an important concern. And if what is contained in these pages is true, it ought to provide some kind of an answer, at the same time confirming the words of the poet when he talked about *beauty* and *truth*, saying they are all that we really know on earth, and ultimately all that we need to know.

The Magic Triangle

You're thinking of getting married? Good for you! You are on the right track! Marriage can really be good for people. It helps keep families going, for one thing, and it can also eliminate a lot of loneliness and boredom in your life.

But be careful. Don't rush into it. There might be dangers ahead! Be sure you have thought things out carefully and know what you are doing. Right now you love your partner, you have talked everything over, and you are sure you're ready. But here are a few pieces of advice that might help you.

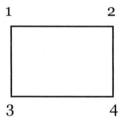
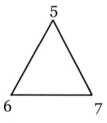

To begin with, think of a square and a triangle. The square has four points, the triangle three, and the two figures together add up to seven points. Also visualize different ways you can put the square and triangle together, two of which are shown below.

But why talk about squares and triangles, you ask. What does all of this have to do with getting married?

Actually, when you think about it, the seven points of the figures represent the basic categories of societal life and everyday living. Almost everything you do might be classified under one of these seven headings: social, economic, religious, physical, aesthetic, intellectual, and political. Keeping these in the back of your mind can often help in solving problems. They provide a good frame of reference within which to sort things out and gain new perspectives.

All of the categories are important, but when you get married, you might want to prioritize them into what you think is the right order. If you don't, your marriage could end up looking like this, everything precarious and insecure. On the other hand, by planning more carefully, it should turn out in a different way. If you put first things first and concentrate on what you are doing, you can build a happy home for yourself.

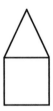

Of course, it is always easy to oversimplify. The

main thing is to stay realistic. Marriage is important and worthwhile, but it certainly is not always easy. It definitely takes planning and effort to keep it going. Anyway, here is what the two figures might look like when they are labeled and filled out.

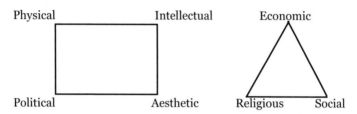

Both figures are necessary, but one much more than the other. Just remember that it is the triangle that will usually pull you through a good marriage, and not the square. This does not mean that the points of the square should be taken lightly. The *physical* aspect, for example, is extremely important. Happy marriages depend a lot on people staying healthy and taking care of themselves, practicing good physical hygiene and eating the right foods. Your marriage might run into real trouble if you are sick or tired much of the time, or if you do not keep yourself clean.

In regard to the *political*, there is not too much to say, but a good marriage does depend on the *aesthetic* and especially the *intellectual*. Think carefully about these two areas and try to choose the right person for a mate. Be sure you marry someone that you feel is your equal and with whom you have at least certain things in common. People say that couples get along well sometimes even though they are very different, which could be true. But be careful! It might not be worth taking the chance. In the long run, it definitely helps when marriage partners agree on many things which are aesthetic and intellectual, and maybe at times even political.

And then, after all of these, there is the magic triangle! The shape of the figure itself is impressive and encouraging, particularly when it is turned the right way. It symbolizes a good foundation, hope for the future, and a positive sense of direction. Each of its three points is extremely vital and important!

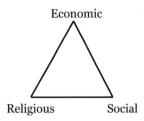

First, there is the *economic* aspect: earning money, buying food, renting an apartment, and paying bills. It is difficult to overemphasize the importance of going into a marriage with a good job or at least the reliable guarantee of one. Many young couples run into trouble early because of things pertaining to economics.

Having a dependable job, one that provides an adequate income from the beginning, and also one that you enjoy, should be close to number one in priority. Once again, as you prepare for marriage, think about economics carefully. You love your partner and have talked things over, and you think you are ready, but do you have a good job or the certain prospect of one? If not, you might want to try an experiment.

Living together before marriage is not a good way to begin. A strong, healthy society is not built on this kind of principle. But it might not hurt to go through the motions and routines of marriage for a few months to be sure you are able to do it. Plot out exactly what it takes to finance monthly living to see if you are capable of earning enough money to cover it, preferably with some left over.

And again be sure you like your job, even if it is just temporary. Sometimes you might be going to school in order to acquire additional skills, or maybe you are working for promotion to a better job or position. In the meantime, try to like what you are doing because you might be with it for quite a while.

The next aspect of the triangle is the category of *religion*. It is a point that is often neglected, or even avoided, by people giving counsel and advice. But like economics, the importance of the religious aspect of marriage can hardly be overemphasized.

It makes sense that religion should play an important part in a marital relationship. In general, couples will have an advantage from the beginning if they believe in God and respect him. This respect will not only carry over to one another but to children born into the family as well.

It is ironic that sometimes the older and more mature a person gets, the less religious he becomes. As a child he has a simple faith in God, but later as an adult he becomes more detached and aloof. Increased intelligence and experience result in a corresponding decrease in religion.

Since God exists, and he really does reign over the universe, it is logical that people will fare better in life if they recognize him and show the right kind of devotion and respect. Especially for those who want a successful marriage, this will be an extra security and safeguard which they cannot afford to be without.

And then finally there is the seventh and last category, the third point on the triangle and the one which is possibly the most important of all. This is the *social* aspect of marriage, the ability to relate to someone in a unique way and to fall in love. It is the idea of establishing a certain type of relationship which is different from all others and is characterized by romantic love and intimacy. Certainly if two people cannot achieve this, all other aspects of marriage become less relevant and meaningful.

But how can you be sure about this kind of love, you ask? And how can you depend on whether or not you have it?

Well, first of all, in preparing for marriage, avoid a *whirlwind* courtship and engagement. Give yourself plenty of time to get acquainted, even time to back out if you need to. Get to know one another in the summer, fall, winter and spring, so to speak. Not that the seasons necessarily have anything to do with it, but at least a year of serious courtship might turn out to be a good idea.

It has been said that long engagements are risky. People can get bored with each other before they ever have a chance to get married. And that is probably one of the main reasons for a courtship, to give yourself a chance to get tired and bored ahead of time, if that is the way things are going to turn out. Once again, be careful. Do not rush into things! The main idea is to get well acquainted and give yourself time to *fall in love*!

By the way, what kind of love is really important? Certainly there are many different types, and the kind that someone has for a parent, brother, sister or friend is definitely necessary in regard to marriage. This kind of attraction and mutual respect is vital and needs to be shared with a marriage partner. But the type of love that is especially important, and the one that can often hold a marriage together when a lot of other things fail, is

6

romantic love.

This is the love you pledge in your marital vows to reserve for only one person, the kind of love mentioned in the Bible where it says to be *one flesh* and to cleave unto a husband or wife and no one else. It is that degree of love which implies a closeness more than any other form of friendship. Among other things, it involves a sexual relationship and the kind of love you share with your partner on a honeymoon.

And maybe that is the grand secret: romantic love and physical attraction! No matter what happens, these two things especially need to be valued and protected. They are usually the things that precede a marriage, in the first place, and they are also the ones that can nurture it and keep it going, and sometimes save it if it gets into trouble!

Well, are you are still thinking of getting married? If so, good! Maybe these few pieces of advice will help you.

But remember! Even though all points of the square and triangle are important, some are more so than others. Take two of them, for example: the *economic* and the *social*. Note how they relate to something that a man once said when asked by a friend how he was getting along with his wife.

"Just fine," the man remarked on that occasion. "We are very incompatible." "But that doesn't make sense," his friend said. "Sure it does," the man told him. "I bring home the *income* and my wife is *patable*!"

And possibly that is one of the best kinds of advice that might be given!

Think Before You Marry!

A friend of mine stopped by the other day, and we got to talking about our daughters and how they were doing in their marriages.

"I have one daughter," he told me, "who's finally getting a divorce after fifteen years. She's living alone now and has two of her children with her. Her husband's a real nice fellow," he said, "but they just don't seem to get along anymore."

Then I told him about my two daughters, one of whom is a single parent with three children, and the other divorced and married again.

We live in an age of divorce," I said. "People nowadays find it a lot harder staying together than they used to."

To which he agreed, but as to a possible solution to the problem, at least as far as our daughters were concerned, we looked at things very differently. It turned out that I had one solution and point of view, and my friend had another. "People are falling out of love too easily," I told him. "Couples need to try and keep a stronger romance in their marriages."

He laughed at this. "I don't think so," he answered. "Love is too fickle sometimes. Marriage essentially is a

9

business proposition where the man has his responsibilities and the woman has hers. You just need to stay with it," he said, "especially when children are involved."

We soon changed the subject after that because it was obvious we were far apart in our ideas, but the conversation did raise the question once again as to why so many marriages are failing nowadays.

Another person with an opinion on this subject is a certain divorce attorney who some time ago appeared on television. At the end of a panel discussion, he stated that laws ought to be passed making it more difficult for people to get married than to get divorced. For example, before obtaining a marriage license, couples should be required to complete some kind of instruction that might help avoid future marital difficulties, those including a traumatic experience for both adults and children, as well as costly litigation.

But the questions still remain. What do you tell people about marriage, and what kind of instruction is best for them to hear? What precautions can be taken ahead of time? I know the kinds of things my friend would probably say, but there has to be more to marital success than talking about a business proposition. And in regard to my own views, I admit there is more to it than just romantic love.

So what do you say? What are some comments and suggestions that might be considered to be good instruction? There are probably more than a hundred answers to such a question, but here are ten quick possibilities.

1. Make good use of a courtship. Be sure it is long enough to get well acquainted, possibly at least one year. Try to remove all doubts, if there are any, and feel absolutely certain that getting married to a particular

person is the right thing to do.

Allow courtship to be a reliable test of compatibility. Regard it in many ways as a microcosm of marriage itself, a model or prototype for the years to come. One of the unfortunate things about married life sometimes is that people change and no longer do the things they found enjoyable during courtship and the first part of their marriage.

2. Get well acquainted, if possible, with your future spouse's parents. Gain their approval and try to feel at home with them. Ask questions and solicit advice. This kind of relationship can help later on, especially if marital difficulties should arise.

3. Obtain reasonable economic and financial security before marriage instead of waiting until after. Be assured of a good job, one that will provide an acceptable standard of living and preferably health care benefits. Put some money in the bank, and start a savings program that draws interest.

Be careful of the mistake others have made, and that is to try and work too many jobs, go to school, and be a good spouse and parent. Some are able to do this, but many are not. Sometimes it might be best to put marriage on hold for a while until the economic future looks brighter and more secure. In the meantime, continue to enjoy dating and courting.

4. Pay close attention to personal cleanliness and hygiene. Notice anything about yourself which might be offensive to a marriage partner, and vice versa.

Try to stay in good health. The success of a marriage is often affected by an abnormal amount of fatigue or sickness.

5. Be aware of the importance of physical attraction. Since this is one of the main things that prompts a marriage to begin with, it ought to be fostered and maintained. Change with age is inevitable, but be cautious of changes that might adversely affect a marital relationship.

6. During courtship determine if there is a general feeling of equality between partners. If not, maybe a marriage should not occur. Too many times one person or the other eventually tends to become more dominant or submissive.

Avoid feelings of superiority or inferiority. Prepare to live all aspects of marriage equally.

7. Go into marriage honestly. Do not harbor secrets and unresolved problems that might eventually cause trouble. Divulge any kind of information, at least to a marriage partner, that might someday prove damaging to a relationship.

8. Make a strong commitment ahead of time to avoid separation or divorce. This is especially important if children are planned. Even the best of divorce settlements cannot compensate family members whose lives are disrupted by marriage failure.

9. Try to solve problems of boredom or depression prior to marriage instead of after. Strive for social and emotional stability, approaching everyday living in a positive way. A marital relationship can be very challenging at times, and it will be more successful when each partner is socially competent and has a mature outlook.

10. Be ready to encourage and promote a continuing romance, not just during the early years of marriage but throughout a lifetime. This will generally include a strong commitment to participate in a sexual relationship.

The signature that a person affixes to a marriage license, in fact, is a contractual agreement that he or she will do certain things, and intimacy and romantic living are among them. Nothing is more important than this kind of closeness and familiarity. It is the one thing that might hold a relationship together when many other things fail.

Not only is the intimate and sexual part of marriage designed for the purpose of having children but also to create a strong bond between marriage partners. People who lose interest in this kind of romance, or dismiss its importance, omit a vital ingredient in marital success.

Anyway, so much for the ten suggestions. Some of them might work and some might not. But at least they are good possibilities for premarital advice.

As for my friend, I think he would probably agree with most of them, although he might find one or two quite amusing, a little fickle maybe. And yet, who knows? These could be the ones that turn out to be the most important.

One thing is certain. Something is needed to help promote successful marriages nowadays and also curb a rising divorce rate. And if my suggestions do not work, maybe there are ten others somewhere that will!

The Rules of Marriage

If you could give an important gift to a close friend or family member, something of great value, what would it be? What would be of most worth to a person or be the most practical? Obviously any number of things might come to mind, but as to a possible answer how about a happy marriage? More than anything else, including fame, fortune, and good times, definitely a happy marriage! Or at least many people would say so.

Like a lot of other gifts, however, this one is sometimes hard to come by. Too many times it involves problems and difficulties. Marriage is usually one of those things that starts out well enough but too often has an unhappy ending, and consequently there are the inevitable questions: Where did we go wrong, or why was there so much trouble? What could we have done to prevent a separation or divorce?

In looking for answers, of course, everyone has his own views. There are as many possible solutions as there are personal opinions. But when it comes down to what is most basic and important, one answer might well stand out above the rest: *People have trouble in marital relationships simply because they do not follow instructions.* In short, they fail to obey the rules of marriage.

And yet, what are these rules? What are the magic

guidelines that can help couples keep their marriages intact?

First of all, visualize two different sets of information, one labeled Group One and the other Group Two. Each contains values or characteristics that are important to a successful marital relationship, but one of them is also very different from the other, and as a result it contains additional meaning or significance. Only one of these groups, for example, might technically be regarded as the rules of marriage.

Group One

Love	Trust	Respect
Unselfishness	Tolerance	Patience
Kindness	Devotion	Compassion
Responsibility	Loyalty	Honesty

In the first group are some of the basic items pertaining to good human relations. They are the attributes that cultivate a strong relationship between two friends or neighbors, between team members and associates. They are also vitally important to a marital relationship, although they do not relate to it exclusively. For this reason, the items in Group One have only a general bearing on the institution of marriage. Instead of so-called marriage rules, they could more appropriately be defined as necessary qualities of friendship and camaraderie.

In trying to discover where a marriage went wrong, people might say that they have violated none of the items in Group One, or at least not seriously. And maybe they are right. It could be that no one, in regard to this area, is really at fault. Why then, they ask, have we had so much trouble? If we did all of these good things, why is there so much difficulty in our marriage? And as it turns out, the answers to these questions might well be found in the items of Group Two.

Group Two

intimacy   passion   sexuality

Nowhere is there a more explicit statement on the exclusive qualities pertaining to marriage. These three attributes alone are primarily what set it apart from all other social relationships. They are what usually initiate marriage, in the first place, and they are what can strengthen it and preserve it later on. Although they offer no panacea for all marital problems, they still might be the saving qualities when many other things fail.

Yet ironically these are also the same qualities that can weaken and destroy a marriage. In fact, they have often been associated with the number one cause of marital difficulty. As one religious leader put it, after conducting many personal interviews in this area, there is one single reason among all others which makes people want to get a divorce. Sex is usually the first one. They just do not get along sexually. They might not say so in court, or even admit it to their attorneys, but that is the reason.

The very thing that was designed to draw people together and develop a strong bond between them in their marriage often turns out to be the main force that drives them apart. What was supposed to foster a close romantic relationship ends up causing estrangement and alienation! What a paradox and contradiction!

Yet the point is still clear. Even when qualities such as love, respect, and unselfishness are present, the importance of the items in Group Two cannot be overlooked or underestimated. Each of them is important socially and physically, as well as religiously, and when they are observed in the right way, they provide a vital ingredient in marriage.

Certainly the most important precedent for this is the one found in the opening pages of the Bible where God told Adam and Eve to join together as husband and wife. "Therefore shall a man leave his father and his mother," the record says, "and shall cleave unto his wife: and they shall be one flesh." At about the same time he also admonished them "to be fruitful, and multiply, and replenish the earth."

This biblical injunction to join with one another in matrimony and be one flesh puts a man and woman under contract to obey certain basic rules, not only those which are implied in Group One, but more specifically the ones in Group Two since they are what technically define marriage and set it apart. Without the latter, in fact, according to one definition, there is no marriage at all.

Even though a marital relationship is commonly regarded as two people joined together by law in a legal ceremony, a more exact interpretation is one which involves an actual physical union, referred to in biblical terms as *one flesh*. Two people might live with one another for years, in other words, assuming all outward appearances of marriage, yet without intimacy, passion, and sexuality, such a relationship is merely platonic and consequently devoid of many marital benefits.

An unusual example of this is illustrated in a short story about Bill and Susan, two young people who decided to test a proposed marriage ahead of time and in doing so learned a valuable lesson. What they discovered was both surprising and discouraging to them, although it eventually resulted in a successful relationship.

The story begins after the two of them had been dating for over a year, and people were wondering why they never married. They had set a date several times but always postponed it at the last minute, not being sure if it was the right thing to do or if it was the right time. Some of their friends had already married, then decided to separate, and they did not want that to happen to them. They believed it would be better not to marry at all if divorce was going to be the outcome.

"But what will we do?" Bill asked one day. "We can't keep going like this forever. Sooner or later we'll have to set some kind of date and keep it, or else give up and try dating other people."

Since neither of them wanted to do the latter, they decided instead to try an experiment, a plan that was risky in some ways yet one which they hoped would give them a release from their dilemma. And although the story is fictional, it is nevertheless something that could easily happen and at the same time puts across a very important point and idea.

The decision which Bill and Susan finally made was to live together for one year, testing a marital relationship to see if it would work. They agreed to go through all of the routines and procedures pertaining to marriage except one, and that was that they would have no intimate relations with one another, other than their usual kinds of dating. It was a daring experiment, but they decided to try it.

Both of them were conservative in their views and shared the same religious values. In fact, the innocence of their relationship was often an amusing topic of conversation among friends. This did not mean that there was no serious romance between them. It just meant that they had drawn a line as to how far they would go, and in their proposed experiment they were confident they could keep it that way. At least they would try for one year.

The main problem was their parents and family, and also the community. There would likely be opposition and disapproval. They especially wanted to avoid a confrontation with the pastor of their church, so it was important, they decided, to keep everything they were doing a secret.

To accomplish this they staged an elopement, making it look like they had been married in another city. They purchased wedding rings for one another, and Bill fabricated the necessary marriage documents at work. Everything was planned very carefully, and luckily they got their experiment off to a good start without any signs of gossip or public opinion. Then for exactly one year they lived together under the pretext of husband and wife, apparently in perfect union and harmony.

In retrospect, what Bill and Susan did was unusual. It was not the kind of thing you hear about every day. People living together unmarried is not uncommon, but for a couple to go to so much trouble in order to test their compatibility is definitely out of the ordinary. And at first it appeared that their experiment was a success. Yet although both of them were relatively happy and content, having had no quarrels or serious disagreements between them, they decided after all *not* to get married!

They lived comfortably in a new apartment and enjoyed a good standard of living. Each of them had a good job. They attended church regularly and honored their commitment not to have any sexual relations. But something was still not right. Neither of them felt the same as they had done before, and they could not exactly tell why. Yet it was enough to convince them that they should not get married, at least for the present, and this could well have been the end of their story.

So what was the answer? Where did Bill and Susan go wrong? In what way, if any, did they make a mistake? After a year of what appeared to be successful living, why did they finally decide not to marry?

Certainly there could be a variety of explanations, but from a very obvious point of view, the answer is clear! Their experiment failed because it was not a true test of marriage compatibility. Not only was it unusual, but it was unnatural. It lacked the one main ingredient that characterizes marriage, to begin with, and separates it from all other kinds of sociality, and that is the physical and biological union of two people. The exact thing that could have drawn Bill and Susan more closely together and strengthened the bond between them, was the one thing that ended up estranging them to a certain extent and pulling them apart.

Traditionally, when the right kind of chemistry exists between two people, they fall in love. In other words, they feel a natural inclination toward one another that is both emotional and physical. Almost universally there is that unique sexual attraction which makes them want to marry and be together. Once married, however, they need to foster such a feeling in order to keep it going. Otherwise the social environment of living together in a platonic relationship might seriously work to their disadvantage.

Bill and Susan were not trying to test the compatibility of two friends, but that of husband and wife. Each situation, of course, requires a much different method. And as time went by, the young couple eventually discovered that the only real way to test marriage potential is by actually being married!

Their experiment also emphasizes the idea that many people who are presently living together as husband and wife in a legal sense are possibly really not married at all. They go through the outward appearances of such, and in many ways appear to be compatible with one another, but because of a platonic relationship, the principle of living together actually works against them rather than to their advantage. They are not using the right formula for marriage, and unfortunately many of them end up in separation or divorce.

As for Bill and Susan, however, their story did have a happy ending. Eventually they got together again, an event interpreted by family and friends as a reconciliation, and then were secretly married. But this time it was real, as was their elopement to another city!

And although it was still too early to tell, their marriage after one year seemed to be going very well. They lived in an apartment and had a good standard of living. Each of them still had a good job and they attended church regularly. Yet friends and family could now see that there was definitely something different.

There was also an important fact that Bill and Susan learned that they had not known before, and that is that you can never really be sure about marriage until you try it. You can think about it, talk about it, and worry about it, and yet no one can ever be entirely certain that it will work. The main thing is to be sure you are in love to start with and then go into it with as much knowledge and information as possible, as well as a strong commitment.

They also discovered that there are two sets of rules pertaining to marriage and not just one. Being friendly and respectful are definitely important, but as time goes by it is not enough.

Bill and Susan went to a lot of trouble trying to determine compatibility, and maybe what they did was not that bad of an idea. But there are safer and better ways to test a relationship. The most important guideline is simply to obey the rules. The majority of people would probably not go too far wrong if they carefully observed the qualities in Group One and especially those in Group Two.

In conclusion, there are many other things that are also vital and important. More often than not, these are the hidden principles and ideas which exist behind the rules, those that can actually determine sometimes whether or not a marriage is successful. Realistically they might well be called the *deciding factors*. And among them, crucial to the success of any intimate relationship, are the strategic concepts of *equality* and *fidelity*. The significance of these two aspects alone can never be overemphasized!

In regard to equality, for example, much has been said about the male figure being the aggressor, the initiator, and the one who usually leads out. During courtship he is the one who makes the date and takes care of the arrangements, the one who does the driving and pays the bill. But in marriage it does not always have to be this way. Particularly in view of equality and equal rights for women, many of the concepts in courtship and marriage now take on added relevance and meaning.

In order to have a strong marital relationship, it is imperative that both marriage partners equally take the initiative. Both need to promote, as well as endorse, the qualities contained in Group One and particularly the ones in Group Two.

In connection with the latter, the idea that men, as a rule, are more interested in sex than women should be carefully analyzed for what it implies and then be discarded with many other questionable stereotypes. A good example of this is the type of advice given by a certain lady author.

Writing to those who might be concerned that their husbands were more sexually oriented, she explained that this is just another basic male-female difference over which they have no control. Her advice was just to accept it. If God had not given men such a strong sex drive, she said, they might never consent to getting married in the first place.

Yet if this is true, that men by nature are more interested in this part of marriage than women, the question always arises as to why! Why was a man created one way and a woman another? What reasonable purpose does it serve, other than the very questionable one suggested by the lady author?

According to many authorities, including evangelist Billy Graham, there are two main reasons for the romantic and sexual part of marriage. One is to have children, and the other to strengthen the marriage bond. These two purposes constitute an important principle which again receives its approval and mandate from the Bible. Certainly such a principle is as important for a woman as it is for a man, so why would God create the two of them so differently in regard to sex?

The truth might well be that such differences, if and when they do occur, very often turn out to be more cultural and psychological rather than purely biological. And if this is true, the need for equality in marriage becomes even more critical.

Supporting such an idea is the opinion of another author, who is both a social worker and marriage counselor. He believes that the so-called biological differences between men and women, as they pertain to sexuality, might be fewer than previously supposed. New information suggests that many differences have to do with cultural background and individual personality rather than biology. It should be reassuring to couples, he says, when they learn that certain alleged facts in this area turn out to be only assumptions.

Finally, and in close proximity to equality, there is the controversial principal of *fidelity*, a concept accepted by most people as being an important part of marriage and one that denotes faithfulness, loyalty, and reliability. But unlike its antonym *infidelity*, which almost without exception refers to moral unfaithfulness and extramarital relations, the former is very often only partially defined.

The idea of fidelity, for example, goes well beyond its dictionary definition. It is not just a matter of avoiding unfaithfulness, disloyalty, and unreliability but is instead an active exercise of marital responsibility and a genuine interest in keeping the intimate part of marriage alive. It is the concept of promoting, as well as endorsing, the qualities in Group One and especially those in Group Two. Particularly in regard to the latter group, it suggests that the way of doing this is not just dutifully, but with equality and desire.

Intimacy, passion, and sexuality, like a lot of other things, have to be nurtured and protected or they diminish and die. Like a fire, they need occasional rekindling. Certainly it is important to keep them going, not only for the purpose of having children during the younger years, but also to strengthen the marriage bond throughout much of a lifetime and in the process enhance the enjoyment of marital living.

In relation to this, it is also important to regard with caution any signs of major change. Closely related to marital problems, the change aspect is a significant factor in almost every case of separation. It can particularly be a threat to the principle of fidelity.

After people marry, they are naturally going to change in some ways. This is inevitable and also necessary and desirable. People might change socially, intellectually, culturally, and religiously, but one crucial way that they should not change, except by mutual consent, is in the positive feelings toward intimacy, passion, and sexuality. Even when change occurs mutually, it still might not be a good thing for a relationship.

Some older couples whose marriages have passed the test of time might not always agree with this, but the problem is that more and more marriages never reach that stage. Separation and divorce are continually on the increase. The fact remains that marriage usually fares better if it maintains its basic character and goes "according to the rules." When the biblical command was given for a man and woman to be one flesh, nothing was ever said about any kind of decrease or discontinuation.

In summary, therefore, there is one basic thought or idea which gives additional meaning to the many different rules and aspects of marriage. It was inscribed on a sign over the doorway of an old Scottish building years ago, along with a set of strange geometric signs and symbols. The building is gone now, but the words of the sign still continue to express an important message:

"What e'er thou art, act well thy part."

In marriage especially, these few words by themselves contain a vitally important meaning. It would be difficult to more aptly express the idea of fidelity and mutual respect, as well as other areas of marital responsibility. To be a good father or mother is one thing, for example, or maybe a good friend or neighbor, but it is quite another to be an effective wife or husband. Doing well in one area does not guarantee success in the other. It all depends on the part one plays and how well he or she plays it.

It also depends on how effectively people follow directions, how good they are at observing sound principles and obeying the rules. How well they perform on stage, as it were, depends on how well they learn their parts and carry them out. In a way, it is just good theatrics. And although there are many accomplishments that people might have, all of which are worthwhile, the one which leads to a happy marriage could well be the most significant part they will ever play, the one also that will be to them the most valuable and important gift!

The Magic Ring

At the same time that God placed Adam and Eve in the Garden of Eden, he also introduced the concept of matrimony and set up guidelines for its success. From the very beginning he emphasized such things as love, devotion, honor, and respect, all important qualities designed to strengthen a marriage and make it work. These provided a good foundation for a successful marital relationship, yet there was still one other element, equally important and not to be left out. A little bit of magic!

"Therefore shall a man leave his father and his mother," the Bible says, "and shall cleave unto his wife: and they shall be *one flesh*."

God blessed Adam and Eve and told them to be joyful and happy. He also commanded them to multiply and replenish the earth. It was important to do these things, he said, and yet it would not always be easy. Eve would suffer pain in childbearing, and Adam would be burdened with the responsibility of providing a living. The main thing was to remain true to one another and be good parents to their children.

Again to help them do this, God prescribed the basic ingredients for a successful marriage: love, devotion, honor and respect. In other words, a man was to cleave unto his wife and be faithful, and vice-versa. Then he gave them the magic: the ability and permission to be *one flesh*!

In no place is the divine decree more simply or more aptly given than in this final statement. A man and woman joined together in matrimony were entitled to live in close intimacy, not only for the purpose of having children but for the joy and pleasure of marriage. Such a thing was meant to be a safeguard in their relationship, as well as the magical element that could help keep them together.

It is like the tales of old when a hero obtained a magic amulet or ring to take with him on a difficult journey. In addition to his own strength and ability, the charm provided the extra ingredient needed for success, a safeguard against danger and a way of meeting the challenges ahead.

And certainly the magic ring in marriage is no less effective. It is an inherent and integral part of almost every marital relationship. The romantic and sexual attraction between a man and woman has persisted throughout the ages and still continues to be one of the most basic aspects of a person's life. Without it there might not even be such a thing as marriage.

But what exactly is it? As far as marriage is concerned, what is the *magic ring*, and what are some of its benefits and characteristics?

Domestication   In the first place, it is a domesticator. It is one of the important drives or motivations that can help keep a person home. The need to be with someone in a close personal relationship is universal and has always exerted a strong influence on the adventurous spirit. Again if it were not for this basic feeling that most people have, it is possible that very few would ever get married.

Familiarity   It also nurtures familiarity between husband and wife, keeping an intimate connection between them. A sense of estrangement and detachment is avoided. They continue to be marriage partners as well as parents and good friends, and the idea of intimacy and romance is not discomforting to them. This part of marriage is extremely important and without it a couple might eventually end up as strangers.

Spirituality   Because of its close association with the Bible, the ring obviously has a significant religious aspect. One of its main purposes, in fact, is to develop spirituality. It is the idea that sexual living within the bond of marriage can not only draw two people close together, but it can also put them into a closer communion with God. Knowing that they are doing his will and obeying an important commandment can give each one of them a feeling of confidence and emotional security.

Balance   To be *one flesh* implies a close marital relationship, one that is emotional as well as spiritual, and since the time of Adam and Eve it was also meant to be physical. Together, these three elements, used in the right way, can give the right balance to a marriage.

It is very easy, however, to become involved in other interests that interfere with a good relationship. Being preoccupied with hobbies, friends, politics, occupations, church and community service, and even with one's own children might contribute to marital neglect. Yet this is where the enchantment comes in, the spell of the magic ring, and in the process of everyday living it can be an important factor in keeping things balanced and moving in the right direction.

Communication   Certainly an important benefit in connection with marriage is communication, the idea of an open dialogue in discussing problems and settling differences. The difficulty sometimes is how to initiate it and also keep it going.

Although there are many things that might encourage this, the one best suited to marriage is closeness, the kind engendered by intimacy and romance. This type of relationship was designed to create a strong marital bond and provide an atmosphere where communication is more apt to occur.

Habit   Doing something because it is worthwhile is one thing, but doing it also to stay in the habit is another. Both can be equally important, as it is with the romantic part of marriage. A continuing romance is necessary, first because it benefits the quality of a relationship, and second because it helps to keep lovemaking a habit.

Relief   In addition, the magic ring can relieve tension and prevent a lot of anxiety and frustration. Consequently, it is an effective deterrent to many kinds of difficulties. It takes two people to make it work, however, and both marriage partners share in the responsibility.

Nowhere is this obligation more explicitly stated than in the seventh chapter of First Corinthians in the Bible. "Let the husband render unto the wife due benevolence," it says, "and likewise also the wife unto the husband. The wife hath not power of her own body, but the husband, and likewise also the husband hath not power of his own body, but the wife."

In this unique passage of scripture is a reaffirmation of the importance of being one flesh, physically as well as spiritually and emotionally. Without such a condition, the marital union would be little different from many other types of social relationships.

Pleasure Most marriages need a certain amount of sexual pleasure to keep them going, a little mystery and intrigue, as it were. This has always been an important aspect of the biblical mandate for a husband and wife to be one flesh. It is one of the rewards or incentives pertaining to this kind of relationship.

For centuries intimacy and romance have been nature's way of providing pleasure in order to strengthen the marriage bond and perpetuate the species. There are very few exceptions. God himself has made it clear that he does not believe in asceticism nor approve of abstinence as far as marriage is concerned, and even after brief separations, according to the advice in First Corinthians, a couple should "come together again" so that one or the other does not do anything that might lead to infidelity.

Youth People were meant to grow old in body but not necessarily at heart, and sometimes the success of a marriage might well depend on it. One of the best guarantees for happiness and longevity in married life is the continuation of romance. The time of youth needs to be remembered and the idea of a honeymoon perpetuated. The day that a person starts thinking that he or she is too old for romantic living may be the day that a marriage starts going downhill.

The power of this kind of love and affection cannot be overestimated. Both mental and physical health benefit from it. It has been said, in fact, that even in later years, sexual activity definitely improves health and contributes to longer life, at the same time helping to keep people feeling young.

Renewal Finally, the magic ring is important because it has the kind of magnetism that brings two people together, even under adverse circumstances. It is a compromiser and a healer. Along with all of its other benefits, it gives a couple the opportunity to express a special type of love and affection and provides a way for continually renewing their marriage vows.

And the renewal of those vows is important. In its own way, it is a type of ceremony, one with a magical quality that is extremely vital in the preservation of a relationship. It is the missing link sometimes between a marriage that is successful and one that is not. Surely it is like in olden days, during the exploits of a hero, where the use of magic so often proved to be the saving factor.

In the tales of those former times, a hero always benefitted from the power of a secret amulet or magic ring, as long as he used it correctly and did not lose it. Most of what he did was on his own, but there were times when he might never have made it had it not been for the ring.

Also the same is true with marriage. Especially today in a time of rapid change and uncertainty, when divorce rates are soaring, people can use all of the help they can get. Literally what they need, along with everything else, is a little bit of magic to nurture their marriage and at certain times even to save it.

And such a thing can happen if people do their part. If they go into marriage thinking of it as permanent, rather than experimental or temporary, and definitely want it to succeed, the idea of a magic ring will always work when they try to claim its many benefits. Fantasy at that time will suddenly turn into reality. It is also on such an occasion that the popular theme in children's literature will finally come true for couples as they discover more completely how to be married and then live happily ever after!

Jed and Nancy

Jed looked out through the window for a minute and then back again to the picture of his wife on the table. He was in a quandary as to what he should do. It wasn't that he didn't love his wife. The truth was that he would find it hard to live without her. But the way things were right now, it was very difficult!

He thought back on his marriage, one that had lasted many years. It had been a good relationship, but it was in trouble now, and he didn't know what to do about it. To Jed the whole thing seemed so unnecessary. "Things are just too complicated," he thought. "And they really don't have to be. If married people would just act like they were married, they would probably be all right!"

Jed's problem was certainly not a new one. People have been running into it for a long time. It was simply a problem of incompatibility. In this case it pertained to the sexual relationship in a marriage, especially in later years, and the kind of role it ought to play.

A few days earlier Jed's wife had abruptly ended a conversation. "I just don't care about sex anymore," she said, her voice raised but not shouting.

"But you should," he told her. "It's as important now as it used to be."

"I'm sorry," she said. "Things have changed, and I just don't feel that way anymore."

Jed and his wife Nancy had five children, all of whom were either married or living away from home. It was just the two of them alone now, and Nancy seemed to be quite happy. She had more time to do some of the things she had always wanted to do, and it usually kept her occupied and busy. Jed was still working at his job, but he also found time to do more things now that the responsibilities of raising a family were gone. Yet unlike Nancy, he was often dissatisfied and restless.

"You're older now," she told him. "You ought to get some new hobbies and interests. You'll have to do that anyway when you retire. Why not start now?"

The problem for Jed had been going on for over a year. During his marriage, there had been personal difficulties from time to time, but nothing like at present. The situation was confusing to him, and he could not understand it, especially one day when Nancy said that as far as she was concerned, she now felt as close to him as ever before.

On one occasion he decided to talk things over with a friend. "How is your marriage nowadays," he asked. "Is everything all right?"

"Couldn't be better," his friend answered.

"How's your personal life?" Jed asked.

"If you mean do we have sex together," was the reply, "the answer is yes. Why? Don't you?"

That was certainly one of the problems on Jed's mind, and the main thing he kept asking himself over and over was what he could do. What could he do to improve his marriage and get it back to where it used to be?

According to Nancy there was no serious problem, but Jed knew that unless they both felt that way, it would do neither of them any good. Their marriage would just get further into trouble.

Such is the story, therefore, of Jed and Nancy. It might also be the story of Tom and Jane or John and Mary, or any number of married couples nowadays. Unfortunately, it is also a story in many cases of separation and divorce, as well as remarriages.

In Jed and Nancy's case, it turned out that Jed had the answer to his own dilemma. "If married people would just act like they were married, they would be all right!" In other words, when there is romance and intimacy in a marriage, even in later years, things will have a much better chance of working. It is the idea of two individuals living together, not just as companions and good friends, but as husband and wife.

Obviously, marriage is something that is very unusual and unique. It is different from all other kinds of sociality, ethically at least, because of the sexual relationship involved. This kind of union was established by God himself, and he did it for two main reasons: (1) the bearing and raising of children, and (2) strengthening and preserving the marriage bond. There was also an important religious factor.

As a consequence, the principle of sex has been strongly inherent in marriage from the beginning. It is a certain amount of intimacy and romance which leads to a marital union, in the first place, and it is the same thing that can nurture it later on and keep it going. Especially at the first, a healthy sexual relationship is probably the most basic thing that can draw two people close together, spiritually as well as physically and emotionally, and as a marriage progresses and matures, the same principle applies if people do not tire of it but try to make it a permanent part of their lives.

The old saying that *what is important today should also be important tomorrow* does not always hold true, but as far as a good marriage is concerned, people probably would be more apt to succeed if they would live according to the basic purposes and agreements set up in the beginning. This includes the concept of a sexual relationship. Those not feeling comfortable with such an idea would probably be better off if they never married.

In Nancy's situation it was a matter of accomplishing one purpose in marriage and then giving up on the other. She raised a family and was a good mother, but she did not carry through completely in her role as a wife. She obviously felt justified because she was getting older and the time for child bearing had passed, yet doing what she did was undoubtedly a mistake. In a very real sense, she broke a marriage vow, just as much to a degree as if she had left her husband and turned her affections to someone else. She allowed herself to drift away and become disinterested in a vital part of marriage!

Certainly no reasonable person would argue that marriage is mainly for sex alone. There are many other aspects, each important in its own way. But on the other hand, no one should ever underestimate the importance of sex either. In marriage there is usually an unwritten agreement that people will do certain things, and one of them is to share a sexual relationship. Not only is it a right and privilege but also a responsibility, and as long as marriage is going along in a normal way, it is not up to one person or the other to decide unilaterally that such a relationship should come to a close.

From a religious standpoint, it is interesting that there is one place in the Bible where just such a problem is discussed. It was during New Testament times when the Apostle Paul wrote an epistle to certain people living in Greece. On that occasion, as recorded in the seventh chapter of First Corinthians, he counseled each man to have his own wife, and each woman her own husband, and then added the following advice. "Let the husband render unto the wife her due," he said, "and likewise also the wife unto the husband. The wife hath not power of her own body, but the husband: and likewise also the husband hath not power of his own body, but the wife."

Nowhere else in scripture is such a concept so clearly discussed and clarified. And in no other place is marital responsibility in regard to an intimate relationship more specifically stated. In marriage, under normal conditions, a woman does not have the right to decide that a sexual union should end between her and her husband, and vice versa, unless there is mutual consent. Even then a couple might need to be cautious, lest such a decision eventually jeopardize their marriage.

In Nancy's case, however, whether or not she would agree with this is an important question. In trying to win her over in the future, Jed will definitely have his work cut out for him. It might take a while, and certainly it will not be easy. Living together as husband and wife can sometimes be very complicated and challenging. But if it does turn out that he is successful and can bring about some kind of mutual understanding, he will undoubtedly end up saving a good marriage. And in the type of world that people live in today, very few things are more important!

Marriage and Chastity

Observing the *law of chastity*, which prohibits any sexual relations outside the marriage bond, is usually a personal matter for someone who is single, but for one who is married it becomes much more complicated. A married person, for example, might live an exemplary life by the usual standards, but if his or her attitude in regard to sexuality should have an adverse effect on a marriage partner, one that influences the latter to break a moral law, both parties could end up responsible.

Consider the situation of a man named Ted. A few years after his marriage, he became busy and involved at work and unintentionally neglected responsibilities at home. He rationalized that he was only trying to make a living and provide for his family, but as a consequence, his wife became interested in someone else and eventually broke the law of chastity.

Or there is a woman named Jane who after thirty years of marriage, when her children were raised, gradually lost interest in having an intimate relationship with her husband. She still loved him, she said, but no longer in a sexual way. Eventually he also turned to another person and violated the same law.

In each of these two instances, some might argue that only one person was actually at fault, and the other should have known better. Both failed to observe good marriage principles, yet only one technically broke a moral law. Others might say that all four failed to keep the law, two of them directly and the other two indirectly. And so who is right? Where is the line to be drawn as far as infidelity and adultery are concerned?

Certainly a logical answer would be that more than one person is involved in this kind of situation. It is more than just a matter of neglect when either the husband or the wife fails to live up to certain marriage vows and specifically does not show enough romantic interest and attention. Or at least that is one point of view.

In marriage there is a unique contractual agreement which commits two people to mutual love and respect, and an important part of that agreement is the admonition, as well as permission, to participate in a sexual relationship. It is a vital and inherent part of matrimony and an implied condition in almost every marriage. Even more important, it is a divine gift, one that should not be abused or neglected. Evidence of these principles is found in the law of chastity itself.

One of the definitions of the law is that *a married couple will have no sexual relations except with one another*. The wording is brief and to the point, and the meaning appears to be uncontroversial. Yet in this particular context, the word *except* has unusual significance. It contains an implication that is too often overlooked.

In essence, the law is really saying that a couple will have no sexual experience with any other person, but as part of the marriage covenant they *will* have it with each other. Not complying with this principle, for whatever reason, could well be an instance of not keeping the law of chastity!

This means that Ted failed to keep the law because he neglected responsibilities at home and influenced his wife to be unfaithful. The same was true with Jane when she allowed herself to lose interest in the intimate part of her relationship, thus causing her husband to turn to someone else. In these situations the offense of one marriage partner might or might not be as serious as that of the other, but the responsibility for it in varying degrees must still be shared.

Part of the difficulty is that people are not always aware that there are two sides to every law or commandment. In other words, there is the *do* part as well as the *do not*. Consequently, someone might never break a law, but he or she might not always keep it either.

Observing, or not breaking, the law of chastity, for example, means not having any kind of sexual relations except within the marriage covenant. Keeping the law, on the other hand, can mean something quite different. It involves doing all of those things which are necessary to prevent any kind of infidelity. Specifically it means fostering a good sexual relationship in marriage—not just giving it an endorsement, but also promoting it.

Many people would never think of breaking a commandment, especially one pertaining to chastity. *Doing something they know they should not do* is basically against their nature. Yet it is the other part of the law that might be a problem, the situation where they fail to *do things that they should.* Obviously, any kind of negligence which adversely affects a marital partnership would be in this category.

It all comes down to a very important principle, therefore, one that is at the very center of obeying this particular law. And that is that people need to *keep* the law as well as *observe* it, making sure that they do not neglect one or the other.

Marriage is a very worthwhile thing, but it can be extremely challenging and complicated sometimes. It is the type of social relationship that people need to enter very carefully as well as knowledgeably. One person alone cannot make it work. Both husband and wife have to work together, especially as far as chastity is concerned. It is as though one were saying to the other, "You help me keep the law, and I will help you!" For one person or the other to neglect this intimate part of marriage is to place an unnecessary strain on a relationship, and it often encourages resentment and dissatisfaction. It also underlines the idea that it is not up to one person alone to decide if and when such a union should end, except by mutual consent. And even then, it might not be good for a marriage.

What is more important is for someone not to allow himself or herself to lose interest, to *burn out*, as it were. Both marriage partners should try to stay in love, continue finding one another physically attractive, and always think of the other as the number one person. These are definitely among the qualities that can help keep a relationship alive!

When God placed Adam and Eve in the Garden of Eden, one of the first things he did was to involve them in a marital relationship. He told them to cleave unto one another, to be faithful, and to be one flesh. This was the natural way. It was the Lord's way.

He knew that marriage would not be easy. He knew there would be difficulties. That was one reason he gave them a sexual relationship, so that along with having children they could also come together often and stay close as husband and wife. It was meant to be a source of pleasure to them and a way of helping them remain true to their marriage vows.

In the much-publicized material found in the seventh chapter of First Corinthians, the Apostle Paul summarized this very well. "To avoid fornication," he said, "let every man have his own wife, and let every woman have her own husband. Let the husband render unto the wife due benevolence, and likewise also the wife unto the husband." Then while reminding the people of further marital responsibilities, he encouraged couples to love one another and cautioned them against being separated for too long at a time. "Come together again," he told them, "that Satan tempt you not for your incontinency."

Certainly for most people, the best way to keep the law of chastity is just to be happily married. Nowhere is there a better guarantee. Very often strength is found in numbers where people join together in a common cause, but where chastity and fidelity are concerned, the most important safeguard continues to be a strong marital bond between two people, namely that of husband and wife. It is nothing more than the biblical mandate given to Adam and Eve in the Garden of Eden.

Such an imperative, unconditional and uncompromising, has always been an important principle. Throughout the ages it has been a divine gift and promise. And in a modern world where there is almost every kind of problem and challenge conceivable, it still is!

An Ounce of Prevention

One of the hardest things to do sometimes is trying to save a marriage that is in trouble. You might be a doctor, a marriage counselor, a parent or friend, but whoever you are you can easily find yourself up against a wall when it comes to talking someone out of separation or divorce.

When people become discouraged and depressed about their marriages, it is difficult, if not impossible, to convince them that they should stay together and try again. "Time for that has passed," they say. "We have tried too long already. Nothing is going to change now, and it is time to bring things to an end." All of which makes it more important to help them *before* they get into trouble instead of waiting until *after*!

Yet the big question is what to say and how to say it. And should you say anything at all if everything seems to be going the right way?

It is nice to know that there is connubial bliss in the life of a good friend or son or daughter, or even in your own marriage. Marital trouble might be the farthest thing from your mind. But then suddenly it is there! Already it is too late to think of prevention anymore, and the only thing left to do is try to find a cure, and that is never easy!

So what can a person do to help keep a marriage

healthy? What is it that might prevent trouble from happening, even in the very beginning? Is it mutual trust and respect? Economic well being and financial security or a set of strong religious values? Or is it just the determination to keep trying and somehow make things work?

Definitely all of these are important, but the one main element that so often holds a marriage together and helps make it successful is still something else! It is the thing that is present in a marriage to begin with, and it is the main factor or condition that can keep it going. Simply, it is a strong romantic relationship which exists between a man and a woman.

You can talk about all kinds of formulas and solutions, including love, honor, and respect, and also the undisputed importance of having a good job and being financially secure. But unless there is a strong romantic influence in a marriage, one that gives it a little *mystery* and *intrigue*, it might turn out to be little more than just two people living together.

There are times when a couple might genuinely love and respect one another, making excellent friends as well as capable mothers and fathers, yet so many times their marriage is not what it could otherwise be because at some point along the way someone has lost the feeling of romance. One or maybe both partners have allowed other things to take precedence over that which they probably valued very highly when they first got married.

It might be that a woman becomes preoccupied as she looks after children and necessarily has less time for her husband. Or a man gets so interested and involved in his occupation that he no longer pays as much attention to his wife. There are undoubtedly many different explanations or reasons, each one being a potential source of marital difficulty.

Little by little, two people drift away from each other. More and more they become separate individuals. They might still retain a genuine love between them, but in a very real way they also allow themselves to fall out of love romantically. And so again, what is the right kind of advice? Specifically, what is it that a couple can do to preserve an intimate and romantic relationship in their marriage, from the time of youth to the middle years and even into older age? What kind of answer might be given?

One such answer, of course, can always be found in the religious context of the Bible, in the place where it talks about the first marriage in the Garden of Eden. When Adam and Eve were married, for example, God told them to cleave unto one another and be *one flesh*. In other words, he wanted them to join together both physically and biologically. This instruction was very brief, yet it comprised all of the main aspects of a successful relationship, including love, affection, unity, and the important aspect of fidelity. In addition, it suggested a special kind of union and closeness that was meant to be unique to marriage itself.

More particularly, the instruction involved an intimate physical and sexual union between two people. This was for the purpose of having children and creating a strong bond of affection between husband and wife. There was also the idea of spirituality. Without this kind of relationship, marriage might be nothing more than close friends living together under the same roof and working mutually toward common goals.

It was also intended that marriage should be intimate and romantic. God himself put urges and drives inside people so they would think and feel this way. At the same time he also told them to be true to one another and avoid infidelity and adultery.

Is this the answer then? A strong physical and sexual bond between a husband and wife? Is this the secret of preserving a romantic relationship in marriage? The answer is definitely *yes!* At least one of them!

And yet obviously it is not as easy as it sounds since there are so many people nowadays with marital problems. Romance is not always something that just happens naturally. It needs to be carefully planned and negotiated, especially after the honeymoon is over and people start settling down to the process of everyday living.

In conclusion, therefore, there are at least four specific suggestions pertaining to the idea of romance that might help build a successful marriage, and even save it if it is in trouble. Each of them begins with a letter which is part of the word *CARE.*

The first of these is CONSISTENCY. Try to be the same type of person from year to year, basically the kind that you were when you first got married. Two people usually marry because they like what they see in one another at the time, so be careful of changes, particularly the big ones. And when they do occur, be sure it is according to mutual consent.

Enjoy life but do not expect too much from it. Be careful with the urge for new experience, and try not to get bored with everyday routine. Especially do not get bored with your spouse! Keep the idea of a honeymoon going in your life, year in and year out, and enjoy the repetition of romantic living.

Number two is ACTIVITY. Do a lot of things together, and avoid too much activity on the side with other people. Try to make your spouse the one main person in your life. You might not always be doing something that is exciting and interesting, but just being together is important.

Also be sure that some of the things you do are intimate and personal, the kind that are separate from family life and friends. The most important index of successful romantic living might well be the amount of time spent privately in the bedroom.

Next is REGULARITY. Do important things on a regular basis. Leaving them up to chance or doing them in a casual way often ends up not doing them at all. There are a hundred other things waiting to compete.

In regard to intimacy, set aside at least one day each week for something specifically romantic. Eat out, go dancing, take a walk in the park, or go to a movie. Do anything that you used to do on a date, and then follow it up later in the evening with romance and lovemaking. Even when there is a large family of children involved, people can still arrange to do these things if they really care and try. And almost every psychologist or marriage counselor will say that it usually works wonders in a marriage!

Number four is EQUALITY. Romance might not have too much of a chance sometimes if you do not feel equal with your partner. This involves not only how you measure up to one another physically, socially, and intellectually, but also how you regard the activities that you share together. If one likes dances and movies, for example, and the other does not, this kind of activity might not turn out to be too romantic for either person.

Again it is the idea of change. During courtship you probably took a close look at such things as likes and dislikes, as well as personality traits, and decided that there was enough equality present to justify getting married. The important thing is to continue doing things equally as well as mutually.

Along with everything else that might be said, therefore, it finally comes down to four main suggestions for romantic living: *consistency, activity, regularity* and *equality.* Four magic words, each beginning with a letter that is part of the word CARE. And if people really do care, they can make all four of these qualities work and in the process gain a very valuable asset.

Remember! There are many things worth saving in the world, such as values, friendship, personal freedom and reputation, all of which are important. Certainly the list of worthwhile possessions is a long one. But not one of them, including job, savings, or income, is worth more than those pertaining to a happy and successful marriage!

A Matter of Rights

"It's really frustrating!" the woman said. "Let's face it. We live in a man's world, and women never will have equal rights. We are still treated like second-class citizens, just like we've always been!" She did not hesitate in giving her opinion, and it was apparent that she had completely run out of patience. She was at a point now where no one could reason with her, and any kind of logic turned her off.

"Nothing you can say will make any difference," she said. "There is no such thing as equality. Women have never been treated equally with men, and they never will be!"

Everyone stopped what they were doing and paid attention, but no one tried to argue with her. Mostly they waited to see what she would do next.

For one thing she complained about her job situation where she had been bypassed several times on promotions. Her income was also considerably less than that of some of the men she worked with, even though they held the same kind of position. In addition, she alluded to certain things which had taken place in her own marriage. Her main criticism, however, was male arrogance and chauvinism. This was the one thing she could not take!

It was why she finally threw up her hands and said, "That's it! I've had enough. This kind of thing is never going to change or get any better. Men have been brought up on a traditional male ego, and they probably couldn't get rid of it even if they wanted to!"

And maybe she was right. Or was she? Is there any kind of reasoning or logic that can stand up against her arguments and successfully refute her claims? Is there anything that anyone might say that would change her opinion? Again maybe, and maybe not, but at least one particular answer, using a historical approach, is worth a try.

Visualize a situation, for example, where a small community of people is huddled together under the threat of approaching danger. It is during an early time period when civilization is still young and traditions are just getting started.

Quickly they talk things over and decide that the most logical course of action would be for the women to stay home and take care of the children while the men go out and try to overcome the problem. Or should it be the other way around? Maybe the men ought to protect the children while the women deal with the oncoming danger.

Obviously, such an event, if it ever happened, was a significant one. It was a situation where some important decisions were quickly and hastily made. Roles for men and women were established, not just for the time being and a few years ahead, but for centuries to come, and consequently historical precedents were set.

"You stay home," the men said to the women, "while we take care of things." Of course, this might have had overtones of male ego and superiority at the time, but for most males in that kind of situation, it possibly amounted to something else. In view of the circumstances, the idea that different roles for men and women naturally fall into place might be closer to the truth. Physically, it was a male responsibility to take care of the danger, and a female responsibility to stay behind with the children.

With an increasing number of women today serving in the armed forces, that role is being altered somewhat, but historically it was almost exclusively men who were on the battlefield. As a result, they were the ones who predominated in the field of work and occupations, although that is another tradition which is rapidly changing.

Still one more role that has undergone change, and which probably had its genesis during ancient times, is voting. As men in an earlier age went to confront a dangerous situation, for example, they undoubtedly had to make certain preparations, such as choosing a leader and deciding on military strategy. In addition, they had to deal with logistical problems.

"Let's take a vote," one might have said, "and decide what's best to do." "How about the women?" said another. "Shouldn't they have a vote? They're a part of this, too." "There isn't time," was the reply. "Anyway, this is a man's job!"

The point is that somewhere and sometime in history, things got started in a man's direction as far as the fields of battle and work were concerned, and once in motion, they just kept going that way. Voting and politics were caught up in the same process. It was not that men were smarter than women, more competent or superior. They were just physically stronger, in general, and roles in society were established accordingly. As a consequence, this resulted in the responsibilities of homemaking and child care being delegated to women.

It was no fault of a man that he was cast into a role of protector, provider, and politician. Neither was it the woman's fault that she acquired the role of mother, homemaker, and caretaker of children. Things just worked out that way through natural processes, and as far as women were concerned, they were possibly very satisfied with the roles which they had at the time. After all, going off to war or working in the fields every day was not necessarily that popular of a thing to do.

It is easy to see, therefore, why the making of history down through the centuries became predominantly male-oriented, and how the term *a man's world* came into being. It also shows how equality and equal rights for women, as viewed from a modern perspective, gradually diminished along the way.

But times have changed now, especially during the last century, and women are increasingly unwilling to continue in their traditional roles. Many have come to believe that complete equality is the only acceptable goal, and that additional changes in the economic, social, and political structure of society, as they relate to women, still need to be made. It is not a matter of *whether* this will occur, they say, but *when*, and sometimes even tomorrow or right away does not seem soon enough! Too much time has gone by already.

Women are demanding equality especially in regard to occupations in the workplace. This includes not only equal job opportunity but equal pay as well. The time has come, they argue, for salary to be based on competence and skill and less influenced by other factors, including gender.

Along with this, of course, there are counter movements and opposition. Men do not easily relinquish the role advantages they have held for centuries but often try to keep things the way they are. They might agree with the principle of equality in general, but only from a traditional point of view. And in doing so, they continue to invite criticism from women who regard them as domineering, and often chauvinistic, unwilling to accept equal rights completely because of a male ego.

Yet history is always a controlling factor, and men are merely doing what they have been conditioned to do. At an early age, for example, a young boy learns that he should be kind to girls, not rude and impolite. He should be their helper and protector. At the same time, because of this superior role or self-image, a boy tries hard never to be outdone by a girl, especially in physical activity and sports. He also tries not to cry so that people will not view him as being effeminate or call him a sissy.

This means that in the life of a young boy, the emphasis lies heavily upon male dominance, mainly based on tradition and physical superiority. From the beginning he is brought up with the idea that he should act in a manly way and always protect the *weaker sex*. It is no wonder that he should later enter the fields of work and politics with these same kinds of feelings and attitudes. They are a natural consequence of how he has been raised, and the point is that he should not be overly criticized for them when they conflict with women's rights.

In the place of criticism, women might try showing sympathy sometimes, and even pity, in situations that occur. Psychologically, this is a smart thing to do, if for no other reason than to keep things in a historical perspective. Such advice is easily given, however, and putting it into practice might not be so easy, particularly in the wake of all that has happened.

Certainly from a female viewpoint there are few things more objectionable than an arrogant and chauvinistic male confidently going his own way. This is especially true if he is in an administrative position. His apparent egotism and self-confidence are not only offensive but repulsive. Yet in reality such an individual might be relatively insecure, and his outward manner merely a coverup or an attempt to successfully live up to a role.

Actually, what it maybe comes down to is a woman's ego against a man's, and in view of the way things have developed historically, each would probably be wise to sympathize with the other rather than criticize. Also women might remember that chauvinism and arrogance are not always strictly male characteristics.

In conclusion, it is meaningful to relate this type of subject to the concept of marriage, particularly as it involves romantic living, intimacy, and sexuality. It is especially significant, in connection with equality and human rights, to speculate how male dominance over a long period of time has affected female attitudes toward sex.

The tendency of women to be less motivated regarding sexual relations, for example, if in fact this turns out to be true, is very likely a direct consequence of how they have been treated down through the years. It is the idea of not being equal in one thing as a result of not being accepted as an equal in another. And in regard to employment and occupations, the opinion of the woman who spoke out vehemently at work that day was that those of her gender have never been on an equal basis with men and never will be.

The fact that women have so often been held back

economically, politically, and socially has certainly not encouraged them to be as active and aggressive in sexuality as men. It is not so much that they were made that way, either biologically or psychologically, but rather they have been conditioned to be so. For centuries women have been culturally suppressed as far as marital sex is concerned, and only during the last one hundred years have there been any signs of significant change.

It is easy to see why the woman at her workplace was perturbed over male arrogance and chauvinism. This was the one thing she could not take. Is it any wonder, therefore, that she and other women like her might not always react equally with men in relation to intimacy and romantic situations? Are there not important reasons why they might typically be more cautious and withdrawn, particularly in view of sexual harassment and the traditional concern for such things as rape, physical abuse, and assault?

In this regard, the woman at work was probably right. Men have been brought up on a male ego, and they sometimes could not get rid of it even if they wanted to. They themselves are the product of cultural conditioning.

Yet one idea still stands out from all of these different factors and circumstances, and that is that within a successful marital relationship, there is an opportunity to override many of the social problems existing between men and women. If there is one main place where it can occur, this is it. The important thing is for there to be a mutual feeling of equality and trust, one that encourages a sharing of marital responsibility and at the same time an equal exercise of initiative.

As to the woman at her work, whether or not she will ever resolve her job problems, as well as those in her own marriage, is another question. Some believe that such things are just part of human nature and will more likely go on forever. Certain male and female differences will never change, they say, and the best thing to do is just learn how to cope with them.

And yet definitely there is the other viewpoint. By way of a strict standard of *equality*, a married couple can bypass many such differences or at least turn them to their own advantage. Through a unique type of partnership, they can achieve a high degree of satisfaction and happiness. Especially in regard to intimacy and sexuality, the common bond between them as husband and wife can promote, as well as endorse, this important part of marriage.

In such a situation, there is seldom any confrontation with chauvinism or an arrogant attitude. Equal rights and equality are far from being an issue. Instead, it is two people living together with a definite philosophy and point of view, a way of living that not only gives them compatibility in their relationship but at the same time provides additional security and a more optimistic outlook on married life. And when it comes to a reward worth working for, such a one is hard to beat!

Honeymoon Revisited

"What can I do to save my marriage?" "How can I develop a better relationship with my spouse?" Familiar questions? If not and you're married, you are lucky!

There are a lot of people nowadays who are asking these questions, or who maybe should be instead of hurrying off to a divorce court. Something has gone wrong. Things are not what they used to be. Somewhere along the way their marriage has changed, and it is not always easy to tell why.

Very often the reasons for such a breakdown are obvious, including finances, personality conflict, alcoholism, and abuse. These are just a few of the many possibilities, especially finances! If people do not have a good job and enough money to live on from month to month, it can turn out to be a real problem, and until it is solved, everything else might have to wait its turn.

But if finances are not the reason, one of the main causes of marital difficulties is that people simply do not remember what it was like when they first got married. Or if they do remember, at least they do not feel that way anymore. If there was just some way they could turn back the clock and try to be more like they were in the beginning, the situation would quickly improve.

"But that's too simple!" you say. "Things are not

that easy. In real life it just doesn't work that way!" And maybe this is true, but still it is worth a try!

Think for a minute. What was it really like when you first got married? What caused you to make such an important change in your life? Along with whatever else you might say, here are some typical responses. See if any of them sound familiar.

"It just seemed like it was time for a change." "I wanted to settle down and raise a family." "It was too hard living at home anymore." "My wife's father talked me into it."

"It was difficult being alone all the time." "I just knew it was the right thing to do." "Two people can live together for the price of one." "I felt like the world was passing me by."

Typical answers? Well, maybe and maybe not. But these are things that people might possibly say, at the same time bypassing the *real* reason why most of them finally decide to get married and that is that they merely fall in love!

"Oh, fine!" you say. "So what else is new?" Yet it is true. There is a variety of things that might attract people to one another and cause them to consider getting married, but by far the one that convinces them that they should actually do it is the phenomenon of *falling in love*.

Which means what? Adoration, respect, affection, compatibility? Yes, but there is still more. Love itself usually comprises all of these things, but falling in love implies a separate and more exclusive meaning. More specifically it might be defined as a strong *physical attraction* between two people which makes them want to be together in a more intimate way.

It is as though each individual has a switch or controlling device inside, and when he or she becomes acquainted with the right person, the switch turns on. This is physical or sexual attraction, and without it most people would probably never get married. They might look favorably upon the idea of having children and raising a family, and many other such things, but the majority of them would seldom marry for these purposes alone.

Once again, when it comes to a logical and realistic answer, the main reason why people usually agree to marry is because of this strong physical attraction. It is the process of *falling in love*, definitely separate from love itself which has a much broader meaning.

And this is the thing that can revitalize and rejuvenate a troubled marriage later on! Two people merely need to fall in love again. They need to try to find one another desirable and physically attractive like they did when they first got married and went on a honeymoon. It is a matter of turning back the clock to the way things used to be in the beginning.

"But maybe it's too late," you say. "Maybe so much has happened that people really don't want to go back."

Which might be right! Yet that is also the grand secret! It turns out to be a genuine test to see how interested people really are. But if they seriously want to save a marriage and improve their relationship, this is the best way to do it because there is such a strong precedent for it. They know that things once worked for them to begin with, and if they follow the same basic formula, it will probably work again.

And when a person says, "I love my wife" or "I love my husband, but we just can't get along anymore," the answer again is that even though they have a certain love for one another, they still need to do what is necessary to repeat the process of *falling in love!*

Sounds crazy? Just a jumble of words and mixed-up semantics? Well, maybe, but that is the kind of world we live in nowadays, and the formula for improving a marriage, especially if things like finances are not the problem, is still pretty well defined. *Try to do things more the way you did when you first got married!*

And that includes the honeymoon! The thing uppermost in most people's minds on their wedding day, after the ceremony and reception are over, is going on a honeymoon. Few people will dispute this. It is a very traditional event and one also that is healthy and natural, and if everything goes as planned, the marriage gets off to a good start.

Typically, a honeymoon will last from one day to several weeks, and then years later a couple might go on a *second honeymoon.* But one of the secrets of a happy marriage, regardless of many other things that take place, is to keep the idea of a honeymoon going week after week and year after year from the very beginning.

What it really amounts to is a healthy and romantic attitude toward sex within the institution of marriage! This is something that needs to be perpetuated, not only for the purpose of bearing and raising children but for the preservation of marriage itself!

The day that a person starts losing a physical attraction for his or her spouse is the day that a marriage can easily start going downhill. The old cliche then becomes a reality. The honeymoon is really over! Yet it does not have to be this way. If two people are genuinely interested in preserving their marriage, they can usually do what is necessary to keep it going.

The problem is that sometimes a marriage partner gets bored, and he or she begins looking around for new experience, turning romantic attention to someone else. Others become preoccupied in other ways, becoming distracted from marital living. They get involved in new types of activity or become hampered by tensions and pressures, even ideologies, that affect their attitudes toward sex. Certainly the different types of problems are many and varied.

But the answer to a successful marriage is still very clear. Do not just love your spouse, but keep falling in love over and over again! Try to make romantic living an important part of life as it was in the beginning. Keep the idea of a honeymoon uppermost in your mind like it was on your marriage day, and if things go wrong *just keep trying*. Remember that this is something that needs to be nurtured and cultivated and often put back into the right perspective.

Sounds good, you say! But will it work? Maybe it is one of those things that is too idealistic and too good to be true. Maybe it is too late for some people. And again you might be right, but the way things have been going with marriages nowadays, at least it is worth a try!

Sexuality and Spirituality

At a time in modern society when divorce rates are high and more and more families are left with a single parent, the question is often asked as to why. In marriages, with or without children, what is the main reason why so many couples decide to separate?

Undoubtedly there are many answers to the question, but possibly none is more accurate and meaningful than that which is implied in the first few pages of the Bible. It is suggested in a very brief equation and formula located at the end of the second chapter of Genesis. In paraphrase the scripture states that if a man wants to have a successful marriage, he must leave his parents and cleave unto a wife, and in the process become one flesh with her. The same would apply to a woman in regard to a husband. Such a relationship was given divine approval in the beginning and since then has continued all down through the centuries.

Very simply stated, most marriages fail nowadays, or at least run into serious difficulty, mainly because people disregard this biblical equation and stop using the formula. Certainly there are other reasons, but this is the main one.

And yet another question has to do with the equation itself. *Leave + cleave + one flesh* equals a successful marriage, but what are the definitions of *cleave* and *one flesh*? Are these expressions of important marriage principles in general, or do they refer to something more specific?

Actually there is only one place in the Bible where this question is definitely answered, namely in the sixth chapter of First Corinthians where it equates "one flesh" with *one body,* and possibly the idea of "cleave" with *joined.* The biblical writer in this instance was the Apostle Paul who used a situation of infidelity to put across his point.

"Know ye not," he said, "that he which is joined to an harlot is one body? For two, saith he, shall be one flesh," referring back to the place in Genesis where the equation and formula are first given.

Consequently, when a couple is married, it is more than just submitting to a legal ceremony. Rather it is the process of joining together and becoming one body and one flesh, meaning a sexual relationship. It is this kind of union, in fact, that can foster a successful marriage, even when many other things fail, unless people misuse the formula and disregard the purpose for which it was intended.

And unfortunately the latter too often happens. According to one ecclesiastical authority, for example, the one circumstance which he found to be most common during interviews with couples having marital problems was the fact that they could not get along sexually. There might have been other factors involved, such as financial problems and how to raise children, but the main reason by far, he said, was difficulty within the sexual relationship!

It is not uncommon, in other words, for married

people to tire of one another in a sexual way or not be able to agree on how such a relationship should take place, or even if it should take place at all. As a consequence marriage often fails. No longer is there a desire or willingness to cleave unto one another, as the scripture says, and continue being *one flesh*.

Of course, some will say that more is always involved in such cases than sexual problems, which is probably true, but the implication in the Bible is that the *one flesh* formula, if followed correctly, will still allow a marital relationship to survive despite other difficulties. It is the idea that a sexual union, when kept strong like it was in the beginning, can be a primary factor in maintaining a marriage.

Still at the same time, there are others who advocate very opposite points of view, among them a group which refers to its program as the *New Celibacy*. These are married people who generally choose to have no sex at all. Couples who have finished having families, or those who have never had them, discontinue a sexual relationship on the grounds that it provides a greater fulfillment in life. Through this type of abstinence, they are able to pursue new opportunities and goals, including those pertaining to spirituality.

As one woman has expressed it, a platonic or non-sexual relationship allows her love and spiritual strength to multiply, whereas when she is sexually involved with someone, her energy is drawn away from her spiritual self. Also another woman, in her early forties, says that to prolong sexual life until age 60 or 70 is definitely unnecessary and would otherwise be an imposition on the rest of her life.

Again it is the idea of a couple, or even someone

who is single, embracing a new type of celibacy in order to explore further horizons of the love relationship. For them the entrance to a new stage of life provides additional advantages and benefits. And although this kind of thinking might appeal to a certain number of people, it is nevertheless not God's way.

From a religious point of view, or one that is purely physical or social, the marriage formula in the Bible pertaining to one flesh is still the philosophy that can furnish all of the necessary benefits as long as it is used correctly. Not only was it given for the purpose of having children but also for bonding a marital relationship and keeping it alive and healthy.

Yet too many times the formula is still ignored or forgotten. In a variety of situations and circumstances, one spouse or the other decides that it is time for this type of union to end. No longer is it considered desirable to continue a sexual relationship, and when this happens it very often is the beginning of the end for a marriage. Ironically, the thing that was designed in the beginning to help couples stay together ends up being the thing which estranges them and drives them apart. Even when there is mutual agreement between spouses, marital difficulties can still develop.

What is important, however, is that the biblical formula for marriage does exist, and it continues to be available to people for their use and benefit. In a very realistic sense it is a philosophy that one can choose either to accept or reject. Also as to validity, there has never been a problem since the conditions under which it was given are well-known and its status as a religious principle is unquestioned. Yet in spite of all this, there is still the obvious question as to why the formula does not work better, and why so many people have trouble with it.

Again there could be many reasons or explanations, but the one possibly closest to the truth is that although most people are acquainted with what it says in the Bible, they are not completely familiar with the formula. Something is missing in their understanding of it. Aside from having children and strengthening the marriage bond, there is still an additional factor which is apparently relatively unknown, one creating a type of triangle, as it were. And since the *one flesh* formula was first given in a religious setting, it follows that this third part is also religious.

The concept involved, for example, is that unless a person enters into a sexual relationship with someone within a legal covenant of marriage, he or she might fail to acquire a certain *level of spirituality* that was originally intended. It means that there is a particular point of view or frame of mind in life, however it might be expressed, that people need to develop. Otherwise, the question arises as to why the *one flesh* idea was instituted as a religious principle in the first place.

The meaningful way of regarding sexuality, in fact, is to define it specifically as a *gift from God*. It is a present which he has placed in people's hands for their use and benefit. As such it should be valued and appreciated, but at the same time not abused, neglected, or taken for granted. It is something that needs to be nurtured and fostered from time to time, and very often rekindled, or it can soon diminish and disappear.

Certainly this kind of understanding and appreciation of one's sexuality can in turn increase spirituality, as well as provide the main basis for fidelity and trust in a marriage. It can be the primary safeguard against infidelity and immorality. Knowing that it has this spiritual aspect, along with the two that are physical and social, and also that it has been instituted and sanctioned by God himself, can significantly strengthen a marital relationship.

This is true even in marriages that appear to be highly successful. A couple might have an outstanding family, in other words, and enjoy a strong intimate relationship, yet at the same time disregard or overlook the religious part of the triangle. They might or might not have religion in their lives, but in either case they exclude the spirituality of being one flesh. And without this awareness, a significant meaning of the marriage formula is bypassed, and the occurrence of future marital problems always remains a possibility.

But once more this brings up a question, one that asks why so many people disregard, or are unaware of, this third aspect. Why does such an important principle continue to be obscure and unidentified? And among the possible answers, the most likely is probably because of sex itself.

Without any doubt, there are very few subjects that are more controversial and emotionally charged than this one. Either an aversion or inclination toward this particular topic is found everywhere, and to say that any kind of sex at all is associated with spirituality might sound too much like a contradiction.

Yet beyond any possible misstatement or paradox, it definitely presents a dichotomy. Possibly no other subject contains a more noticeable dividing line, especially as far as religion is concerned. On both sides there are the incontrovertible opposites.

In regard to three kinds of sex, for example, namely *premarital, extramarital* and *marital*, God holds people accountable for two of them and yet blesses them for the other. On the one side, before marriage takes place, sexual relations with anyone are strictly prohibited, but following marriage they become a reward and an incentive. They are not only permitted but encouraged. In one instance, a person's religious standing is jeopardized, while in the other it is enhanced and protected.

Because of this dichotomy, feelings and attitudes formed on the negative side can easily transfer to the other. As a consequence, illicit sex especially might make it very difficult for people to directly associate any kind of sexuality with spirituality.

And yet this kind of association is nevertheless present, and it is an inherent part of the *one flesh* formula and relationship. It is also one of the important factors in whether a marriage either succeeds or fails. Although not a panacea for all marital problems, it still remains true that a strong sexual union between a man and woman, which incorporates all three aspects of the triangle, continues to be an exceptionally strong force that can keep them together.

But again this creates a question, a very important one as to how couples can remain interested, as well as faithful, in regard to the sexual part of their marriage. How can they avoid the point of departure which so often occurs in a marital relationship because of problems pertaining to sex? Surely there are no guaranteed solutions, but an important thought is nonetheless expressed in a simple verse and statement which applies to a wife as well as a husband, and which each of them could profitably ask one another throughout their marriage. It is based on Proverbs 5:18-19 in the Bible.

What kind of person ought you to be?
The kind you were when you married me!

The scripture contains no greater truth:
Stay true and faithful to the wife of your youth!

This is to say that a couple, in order to nurture or rekindle a positive relationship, needs to think back continually on how things were in the beginning when they were first married. If something was good *then*, in other words, it should be good *now*, and if not, then why not? Obviously it is a question that needs to be addressed.

At least it is a way of establishing a meaningful frame of reference in which to look at a problem. It also emphasizes the potential danger of the passage of time with its inevitable changes. The latter especially can be a good thing, but if they do not have the consent of both marriage partners, they can eventually result in negative consequences that can be very injurious to a marriage.

And as far as attitudes and philosophies like the *New Celibacy* are concerned, these are definitely in contrast with the formula and equation found in the Bible. To condone such practices is to interject a monastic kind of asceticism into a marital relationship that was never intended. As implied in the Book of Genesis and also stated by the Apostle Paul in the seventh chapter of First Corinthians, it is much better for a couple to stay together in an intimate way, except for maybe short periods of time, not only for a happy marriage but also to avoid infidelity.

"Defraud ye not one the other," Paul said, "except it be with consent for a time, that ye may give yourselves to fasting and prayer, and come together again, that Satan tempt you not for your incontinency."

It is commendable that the new celibacy movement is directed toward such things as personal fulfillment and spirituality, but all of this is already part of being one flesh as outlined in the Bible, or at least it can be if the marriage formula is completely understood and followed. The important thing is for a person to follow the equation, which is that he shall "leave his father and his mother, and shall cleave unto his wife: and they shall be one flesh." That is exactly what Paul says when he counsels married couples to "come together again" after being briefly separated. He also gives some very specific advice in regard to being one flesh:

"Let the husband render unto the wife due benevolence," he states, "and likewise also the wife unto the husband. The wife hath not power of her own body, but the husband: and likewise also the husband hath not power of his own body, but the wife."

All of this, of course, can be taken in different ways by people who hear it. Some will still say that definitely too much emphasis and attention are being placed on sex in connection with a successful marriage, while others maintain that too little is said about it with the result being an excess of separations and divorce. Again there are contrasting opinions and viewpoints which could go on forever.

But whatever the correct answers might be, one thing at least remains clear, and that is that when the first couple set up housekeeping in the Garden of Eden, they were given some very specific instructions concerning marriage, and since that time nothing has really changed. No valid options or alternatives have ever been given. The best chances for marital success and happiness for those who want to listen still remain very well defined and are found in the *one flesh* equation and formula as recorded in the Bible!

The Red Rose and the White

Upon entering the room, the girl was immediately curious about the roses, one red and one white, both displayed together on a small table by the doorway. They were made of silk, yet they looked very real.

"How pretty," she said, turning to her friend. "They have some kind of symbolism, don't they."

"They do," he told her as he took her coat and gloves. "How can you tell?"

"It's the way you have them arranged," she said. "But what are they? What do they mean?"

"Do you remember reading about the Wars of the Roses?"

"In English history?"

"That's right," the boy said. "The House of Lancaster was represented by a red rose, and the House of York by a white. It was a way of distinguishing between the two groups during their long years of conflict.

"Anyway," he told her, "that's what I was thinking about when I bought the roses, except that mine have social meaning instead of political. The white rose represents *love*, for example, and the red one *passion*.

"Love and passion?" the girl asked.

"It's a type of marriage symbolism," he explained. "It suggests that love consists of admiration and respect, but it's passion that finally makes someone fall in love and want to marry."

It was apparent that the young girl did not totally understand the idea, but at least it gave her something to think about. Certainly it is an idea that has been controversial at times rather than accepted as truth, yet the reasoning behind it is a logical one.

The concept of love can involve many types of personal relationships, in other words, including parents, siblings, and friends, but *falling in love* is something very different. It is like a girl saying that she really likes a boy but is not in love with him, or vice versa, which is the same as saying that genuine friendship exists but without desire or passion. The difference, of course, is what sets marriage apart from all other social relationships.

The implication of the roses was that not only are love and passion necessary ingredients in a marriage, but there is also the potential of conflict if the two do not exist harmoniously. What the boy wanted to put across was that the latter especially was a crucial factor. Without it there would normally be no children and families, and also the bonding process between husband and wife would be adversely affected. In addition, it could have a significant bearing on spirituality.

It is the idea that from the beginning, love and passion were inseparably connected as far as a successful marriage is concerned. Ideologies and personal opinions might vary, but especially from a religious point of view such as that set forth in the Bible, an intimate relationship between a man and woman, including both love and passion, is not only necessary but also indispensable.

Consequently, it is the thing that can weld a relationship together, not solving all of its problems but acting as a catalyst for marital stability and happiness. It is the biblical concept of sexual unity and *one flesh* and the unique system of sociality that was designed to bring couples together in matrimony and then keep them that way.

And yet at the same time there was always the potential for opposition, the possibility that love and passion might sometime succumb to incompatibility. For any number of reasons, one emotion might become dominant and affect the other, a wife losing interest in the sexual part of her marriage, for example, or a husband having passion at the expense of affection. In either case the stage is set for a possible separation or divorce.

The display of roses on the table reinforces the idea that love and passion should complement, rather than hinder, one another in a marital relationship. If a husband and wife consider this fact and do their part, such an arrangement can achieve the purposes that were originally intended for it. Procreation, bonding, and the increase in spirituality can all take place. But again it requires awareness and cooperation.

The secret, in addition to staying in love, is to maintain a continuing interest in sexuality. It means giving serious attention to the important aspects of romance. Again this implies more than just love, however, which is an assumed part of any marital union. It also involves a strict commitment to a lifelong participation in sexual relations to an extent that is agreeable to both marriage partners. And when one or the other begins to show apathy or disinterest, it is then time to rekindle the passion in their relationship.

Yet the question is always how to do this. How can a husband or wife, or both, revive an interest that at one time was strong within them? What are some of the ways that can help renew this important part of marriage or keep it from deteriorating in the first place?

Obviously there are many possible ideas, but to begin with, one approach is suggested in a dialogue between a couple named Tom and Karen. Their conversation does not pertain to sexuality per se, but rather to the related topic of spirituality and religion.

Tom It's been a long time since we've been to church, Karen. Why don't we go this Sunday?

Karen All right. I know we should, although I'm not too much in the mood for it.

Tom You used to like church. What caused you to change?

Karen I don't know. I just got out of the habit, I guess. There have been so many other things to do lately.

Tom It's too bad we can't go every week again, not just because we should but because we want to.

Karen I know. The strange thing is that once I get there, I really enjoy it. But then when I get home again, I get involved in other things.

Tom You ought to try thinking about it more often.

Karen About what?

Tom Church. Try to keep it on your mind more.

Karen I remember I used to.

Tom Why don't you try reading some religious books. Maybe that will help.

Karen I don't know. It seems like whenever I read about

religion, or talk about it very much, it just turns me off.

Tom   I wonder why?

Karen   I don't know. It just does. Anyway, a lot of what you read nowadays is just other people's opinions.

Tom   You know what I think?

Karen   What?

Tom   I think you're scared.

Karen   Scared? Of what?

Tom   Of committing yourself to church like you used to.

Karen   I don't think so. Actually, I think I value going to church as much as I ever did. It's just that I hate to be tied down to going every week. I feel so locked in.

Tom   You go bowling every week. Does that make you feel locked in?

Karen   No, not really.

Tom   And neither would going to church if you got back into the habit of it. I really think you ought to do some reading, Karen.

Besides the idea of reading in order to revive interest in a particular subject or topic, the conversation between Tom and Karen is also important because of its analogy. It points to the close association, for example, which exists between religion and sexuality.

It is probably no coincidence that losing interest in sexual relations is very similar to a decline in spirituality. Both can occur gradually, being affected by inactivity and competition with other interests. Because the two are so closely related, especially in a biblical sense, the forces pertaining to one can be much the same as the other. Even though both areas are important aspects of life, it is easy to neglect them in preference to other activities and interests. They might still be regarded as worthwhile, but whatever the situation, the result of apathy and inactivity is the same. A person simply loses interest and falls away.

Staying in the mood sexually, therefore, is much like maintaining a spiritual attitude. The important thing, especially as far as sexuality is concerned, is for a couple to be consistent and stay with an original agreement or plan. If the idea originally was to make sexual relations an important part of marriage, that should be the model for years to follow. If something is good one year, whether it be sexuality or religion, it ought to be good the next. There can be no argument against things changing for the better, but if marital sex is correct and desirable to begin with, it is logical that it should basically stay that way. The important thing is for a couple to recognize this and see that it happens.

In this regard, and as a supplement to the idea of reading in order to stimulate interest, the following are listed as additional ways of promoting a positive sexual relationship.

1. Try to stay in good health, emotionally as well as physically. Be susceptible to romantic feelings and maintain a healthy attitude toward sex. In Greek mythology, all it took was one arrow from the bow of Eros to instill a feeling of romance. Likewise, in modern-day living, it should require no great effort to attend to the important matter of sexuality in marriage.

2. With a marriage partner, develop a rationale for lovemaking. Be specific in listing those things deemed most important, such as having children, bonding, and spirituality. Make a strong

commitment to stay with your plan unless you mutually decide otherwise.

3. Reach an agreement concerning the frequency of sexual relations. The implication in the seventh chapter of First Corinthians in the Bible is that a couple should come together often, if for no other reason than to avoid discontent and infidelity. The important thing is not to let romantic occasions be too far apart.

4. Always strive for equality between husband and wife. Disregard stereotyped thinking which might hamper a good marital relationship. The idea that men trade love for sex, and women exchange sex for love is a clever slogan to remember, but it is not always true, or at least it should not be. Research and practical experience have shown more and more that the sexes can be equal, and that women especially have attained increased equality in sexuality.

5. Be appreciative of sexuality and intimate relations. Acknowledge them as a divine gift to those who enter into the covenant of marriage. At the same time, remember that such a gift was meant to be used and not disregarded or neglected.

6. Equate sex in marriage with spirituality. Make it an important part of religious life. Accept the fact that it is clean and wholesome, and that not to participate after taking the marriage vow is breaking a serious agreement or commandment. Genuine spirituality, in fact, comprises not only those qualities which are traditional, but also the ones specifically related to intimacy and sexuality.

Again, it is the idea expressed in the Bible that one of the most important things a person can do from a religious standpoint is to marry someone of the opposite gender and with him or her become *one flesh*.

7. Give high priority to those things pertaining to marriage and the family, yet at the same time avoid neglecting one for the other. Being a good parent or grandparent at the expense of attending to marital affairs is an error in judgment that too many people often make.

8. Maintain good communication with a marriage partner. Be able to talk freely about sex and feel comfortable in intimate situations. One of the benefits of a successful marriage is the feeling of familiarity between two people, knowing that there is exclusively one person with whom to experience this unique type of relationship.

9. Be protective of the needs and feelings of a spouse. Avert anything that might lead to abuse. It is not the things that a person does sometimes that are most injurious, but the things he or she fails to so. This is especially true in regard to sexual relations.

10. Accept pleasure as an important aspect of sex in marriage. Regard it both as a gift and a reward to those who rightfully participate in this kind of union.

Finally, in addition to all of this, there is again the idea of reading as a way of improving a sexual relationship. Especially in connection with premarital instruction, it constitutes an extremely important factor. Getting the advice and viewpoint of a good marriage counselor by way of appropriate literature can help prevent many potential problems that invariably lie ahead.

Certainly among these is the problem which might include love and passion, the subject of the two roses that were displayed on the table that day. If these two forces operate harmoniously, in other words, the red rose along with the white, the chances are good that a married couple will be successful. There is never an absolute guarantee, but these two attributes working together can be a very important safeguard.

And like the boy said, in explaining to his young friend who came to visit, it is love that brings admiration and respect, but passion is what eventually makes the difference and causes a person to fall in love!

To Be One Flesh

It has been said that you should marry the person you love, but even more important love the person you marry. The same might be true with other things such as attending church and liking it, or choosing the right kind of occupation and enjoying what you do. This type of philosophy involves a magic triangle, once again, one which includes points representing the *social, religious,* and *economic* aspects of marriage.

Getting married is easy, as is professing a love for one's companion, but the important thing is following through and making it work, doing what is necessary to build a lasting relationship and at the same time finding it enjoyable. Otherwise there can easily develop marital difficulties. In a similar way a person might also have a strong interest in religion at first but then lose it through apathy and inactivity. Or because of some kind of neglect, the job he once liked eventually becomes tiresome and boring.

It is again the idea of observing rules that pertain to a certain subject or discipline. If you obey the rules, in other words, you are more apt to succeed, but if you deviate from them it is easy to fail.

In marriage those rules are pretty well defined. Along with observing attributes of love and friendship, there is always the distinguishing characteristic of cleaving to one's companion and being one flesh, the advice given to Adam and Eve in the Bible. No matter how often a person might minimize the latter or give it only equal status with other things, the fact remains that it is still the most exclusive element pertaining to the institution of marriage. As long as a couple pays attention to this one particular factor, in addition to the religious and economic aspects of their lives, it will constitute their most important protection and safeguard.

Yet people still maintain that way too much is being said about sex at the expense of other matters of equal or more importance. This kind of attention, they believe, tends to distort the true picture and bypasses the main problems confronting a marriage. On the other hand, other types of solutions continue to be ineffective in dealing with marital difficulties, and what is definitely needed might be a return to the idea of *one flesh*.

This unique concept, in actuality, is much more than just an important idea or principle. Rather it is a spiritual law and commandment. Although the Bible does not specifically refer to it as such, the implication in the second chapter of Genesis is nevertheless without question. Reference to a *law of one flesh* is definitely an appropriate use of terminology.

It means that when a couple is united in matrimony, they are not only entitled to have sexual relations but are commanded to do so. Except in very few cases, such a policy is never excluded from a marriage vow nor is it optional. The decree is a divine one, and the consequences of not complying with it might be more significant and serious than many people realize.

For one thing, it emphasizes the importance of

sustaining an interest in romantic living, not just for the purpose of having children but for strengthening the marriage bond. It puts both partners under a moral responsibility to stay in love with one another and to maintain a passion and desire for intimacy and sexuality. This is the express essence of the *one flesh* law. It is the main thing that gives it significance and meaning. It is more than just oneness in purpose, or unity in thought and action, but specifically a physical and emotional joining together of husband and wife.

In a real sense, it might be regarded as a conjugation. Although the word *conjugate* usually suggests creating different forms of a verb, another definition is that of joining two things into one, such as a married couple.

Still another is to unite elements chemically and to pair or fuse together. When marriage is viewed within this context, the true meaning of the term is approached more closely. To be married, in fact, is to be joined physically as well as emotionally, and in another sense also spiritually. It is a biological union of two people in matrimony, hence the common reference to this type of relationship as one that is *conjugal*.

Consequently, when God spoke to Adam and Eve in the Garden of Eden and told them to cleave together and be one flesh, he was specifically talking about sexual relations. It was an activity that he wanted them to practice and enjoy. He especially wanted them to have children and stay together as a family. In addition, he also made it clear that to experience such intimacy with anyone else in a premarital or extramarital relationship would be considered not only a transgression but an act subject to severe penalty as well.

Certainly the intended goal from the beginning was a legal and happy marriage! It was designed to be the most basic unit of society, with the family organization to follow, and at the very center of such a union was the concept of a one flesh relationship. It was the idea of love, honor, and respect and many other similar attributes, yet more definitively, as far as marriage itself was concerned, it signified intimacy, passion, and sexuality!

It was the type of union that was superior to all others, yet one that constantly needed to be nourished and maintained. Such was always an inherent part of the relationship. To stay in love with one's companion, in other words, finding him or her sexually attractive, would come naturally at first, but as time went by it would often require certain adjustments and occasional rekindling. More often than not, a couple would find it necessary to reevaluate their position and return to the original setting of early marriage and a honeymoon.

The ideal is to keep the idea of a honeymoon intact from the beginning. It is like going to church each week so as not to lose interest in spirituality and religion, or staying interested in a job or occupation by viewing it positively and putting in quality effort. Especially it is important to do things regularly and consistently.

In connection with marital relations, for example, one pair of researchers reported recently that many of those interviewed said they made dates for sex on more or less the same schedule each week. Rather than finding it routine and boring, the couples said it was something they looked forward to, being ready for it both physically and emotionally.

It was the idea that most married people enjoy a certain amount of spontaneous sex, but it is not always easy to accomplish. What often happens is that one partner might be in the mood for it, and the other goes along so as not to injure feelings or appear to be less sexual. It was better, according to the research, to make plans ahead of time and carry them out on a regular basis. Regularity and consistency again were important factors which could help keep a relationship going.

This is particularly true with religion and spirituality. Unless they are maintained consistently and systematically, they can easily wane and die. Like sexuality, they might change very quickly, being an important part of living one day and on their way out the next. And in a similar way, a person's job or occupation might be just as adversely affected. Whether it be businessman, housewife, or minister, any line of work can become commonplace and boring if not cared for.

What it amounts to, therefore, is that a couple needs to do whatever is necessary in order to take care of their marriage. Definitely it should be the number one priority. And although there are many suggestions as to how it can be done, the most important among them might well be that which pertains to the principle of *one flesh*. If nothing else, it is the one solution from the beginning that has been specifically outlined and endorsed by the Bible.

Moreover, in addition to the explicit statement commanding a husband and wife to cleave together, there is also the implicit warning of what might happen if they do not. One consequence, of course, is that they bypass the opportunity of having children, but another is to miss the important benefit of intimacy which can significantly fortify and strengthen their marriage.

It is as though God were telling them that if they

obey this particular law, they will develop familiarity and closeness, but if they disobey it, they can easily drift apart. Literally they can end up strangers, which has happened to so many others in the past. People second-guess the Lord as to what will give them a successful marriage, and then when it comes to a final accounting, the one main thing that divides them is an incompatibility regarding sex. In simpler words, they no longer cleave together and obey the *law of one flesh*!

It has also been said that a law exists in heaven for every important gift and blessing, and whenever a person receives such, it is because he or she obeys the law upon which the blessing is predicated. Especially is this true with the biblical law on sexual relations, namely that if a couple wants to enjoy togetherness in their marriage, the *one flesh* option is always available, or if they choose to risk alienation and possible separation, that option also exists.

It is simply a matter of personal choice and selection, and in connection with something as vital as a marital relationship, both at present and in the future, no other decision will probably be more important!

A Theory of Merging Circles

The teacher of a class on marriage principles was nearing the end of a discussion one day, and during his final remarks he made the following comment. "Marriage is a very complicated thing," he said, "and should never be taken lightly."

Although some might have expected him to use the word *serious* instead of *complicated*, still it turned out to be a meaningful statement, one that is particularly true in today's society where separations and divorce are constantly on the increase. In fact, when the class was over, one of the students made a further comment that marriage, in her opinion, was so intricate and complex that it should never be entrusted to those who were unprepared for it, especially the youth and inexperienced.

In this last statement, extreme as it might sound, there is an important implication. One of the things which makes marriage so crucial, in other words, is the idea that many people do go into it unprepared and uninformed. With young people in particular there is a lack of beginning knowledge and information, and possibly also personal commitment.

And yet there is always the question of what it is that a person should know. What kind of information does he or she actually need before entering this kind of relationship, and how might it reduce the complexity of marriage and help solve the continuing problem of divorce?

Obviously the answers to such questions are many, reflecting a variety of opinions and viewpoints. But one that might be seriously considered is described in a theory of *merging circles* which relates directly to married couples.

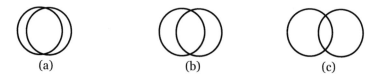

(a)   (b)   (c)

It is the idea that two people anticipating marriage do not necessarily have to be *think-alikes*. In many ways they might differ in their outlooks on life and how they interpret things, and possibly have very different value systems. Yet despite these differences, they can still have a good relationship.

For example, it might be predicted that Couple A has a better chance for a successful marriage than Couples B and C because the first is more alike and has more in common. But according to the *merging circle* theory, it could easily be Couple C whose marriage turns out to be more successful despite obvious differences.

The significant concept in the theory is not how much the circles merge sometimes, suggesting common interests and values, but whether or not the parts that do merge contain certain ingredients. Two things which every couple needs to agree on, in other words, and the ones on which most marriages might eventually depend, can be summed up in two specific questions:

(1) Are you sure that you possess the necessary

qualities of *dependability* and *friendship* for a successful marriage, and (2) are you willing and prepared to enter a permanent sexual relationship?

Theoretically, if a couple can answer these two questions affirmatively, and abide by them, they can usually build a successful marriage. Despite hard times, including social and economic difficulties, these two factors alone can promote a positive marital relationship. And although such a theory might be termed oversimplified and idealistic, it is nevertheless a possibility that is based upon sound principles.

The theory's underlying idea, in fact, is found in the second chapter of Genesis in the Bible where God tells Adam and Eve to join together as one person or one body. This is tantamount to saying that they were formally and legally married and then commanded to have sexual relations. "Therefore shall a man leave his father and his mother," he said on that occasion, "and shall cleave unto his wife: and they shall be one flesh."

At the time, he did not go into detail, such as how to deal with financial crises or economic problems, or how to raise children. He merely gave them a formula for successful marriage and happy living and let it go at that. The idea was that if they would stay together and be obedient to the commandment, other things would be more apt to fall into place.

The directions were that they should not only be faithful to one another, observing the vital aspects of friendship, but they were also to engage in the intimate experience of sexuality. Each of these factors was for the purpose of procreation and spirituality, as well as a bonding process between husband and wife, with the implied promise that if the two were used together, they would result in marital success and stability. This is why Couple C might actually have a better chance for success than Couples A and B, assuming that it has more of the important ingredients than the other two.

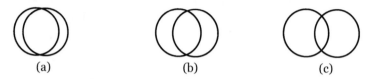

(a)   (b)   (c)

And yet the question still remains, today as well as in the future, as to what people need to know before getting married. Aside from friendship and dependability, what additional information is there that can prepare them for the unique experience of marriage which is characterized and set apart by a *one flesh* relationship? Again there are many answers to such a question, but to those which already exist, the following twenty-five comments and opinions are added.

(1) *The Question of Sex*   Prior to getting married, an engaged couple should make some very definite decisions in regard to sex. They need to decide how important it is and under what conditions it will take place during their marriage. If there is any serious disagreement on the subject, it would probably be better not to marry, or at least wait for a more suitable time.

(2) *Sexual Compatibility*   Couples need to be sure that they "match up" sexually. This is not to suggest premarital relations, which would violate and negate the *one flesh* promise in the Bible, but they should make certain, as much as possible, that there is a strong enough sex appeal between them, one that will be permanent and not just temporary. Going swimming together and observing one another physically, discussing the role that sex will play in their coming marriage, and testing

romantic feelings in appropriate situations are types of activities that can help make a right decision.

(3) *The Honeymoon* Getting off to a good start is always important. The concept of a honeymoon, for example, represents not only an appropriate beginning in marriage, but it also serves as a model and standard for future relations. It is the kind of event that can be repeated regularly and frequently on a smaller scale and can significantly strengthen a relationship. The idea of a continuing honeymoon is the thing that very often keeps a marriage going.

(4) *A Firm Commitment* Often people will remark that a honeymoon is over. A return to work, the task of housekeeping, new challenges and responsibilities, or serious arguments can all create a different atmosphere. Such things are to be expected but potentially they can cause future problems. And yet the fact still exists that a firm commitment to the principles of *friendship* and *marital sex* can be extremely vital to a successful marriage.

(5) *Spirituality* It is important to remember that spirituality is a basic aspect of the sexual process. Certainly it is one that has acquired preeminence in the Bible, since it was God who introduced and endorsed the process in the first place. Along with *procreation* and *bonding*, it is one of the three main elements pertaining to this part of marriage.

If people accept sexuality as a divine gift, in other words, and use it with friendship and respect, and also appreciate it, the implied promise from heaven is that the principle of marriage will usually work. Moreover, by regarding spirituality and sexuality closely together, the marital relationship takes on additional meaning and perspective, a view that fosters fidelity and also encourages couples to participate in sex for spiritual reasons as well as physical.

(6) *Divine Law* Married people who do not have sexual relations are actually breaking a religious commandment. This includes well-meaning couples who for one reason or another choose to become celibate as far as an intimate relationship is concerned. A current movement known as the *New Celibacy*, for example, advocates abstinence from sex on the grounds that it opens up additional meanings in life and provides an opportunity to explore new relationships, including more personal freedom and increased spirituality. It is a way for a married couple to experience a greater degree of fulfillment and satisfaction.

And yet this is not God's way. For very express purposes, he instituted a *one flesh* type of marriage, and any deviation from it is a violation of religious principles and divine law.

(7) *Pleasure* Marital sex was meant to be pleasurable. It was part of the original plan that couples should enjoy one another's company in this particular way, at the same time having children, strengthening the marriage bond, and developing spirituality. The idea of pleasure has always been important within a religious context. It was for this purpose that a climactic orgasm was built into the sexual act, a unique and pleasurable experience that encourages couples to come together often.

(8) *Mutuality* The thing that breaks up many marriages, if not most of them, is an incompatibility pertaining to sex. Either the husband or the wife, or both, will eventually decide that a sexual relationship should end. Obviously it is not uncommon for such a thing to happen.

But if couples decide ahead of time, in regard to sex as well as other things, that they will observe the principle of mutuality in making important decisions and changes, it will usually help in avoiding troublesome circumstances.

(9) *Interest in Sex* Maintaining interest in marital sex is not always easy. Even though nature has provided important incentives and rewards, this kind of interest can nevertheless wane when in competition with work, family, church and community affairs, and a variety of other things. There are different ways that people can continue to be sexually active, however, and it is up to each individual to discover what they are.

It is necessary, for one thing, that couples continue to think about one another in a sexual way. At the same time, even as they grow older, they need to keep themselves comely and well-appearing, representative of how they were on their honeymoon. In other words, physical appearance should continue to complement sexuality. The most important tribute that a man can pay his wife, according to one marriage counselor, is that he finds her sexually attractive, and the same might apply to a wife in regard to her husband.

(10) *Gender Differences* In regard to sexuality, men and women are often characterized by certain basic differences. A man is allegedly more active and aggressive, for example, whereas a woman tends to be more noncommittal and reserved. Also men are more quickly aroused, while women traditionally appear to be on a slower time schedule. And whereas many such allegations are maybe justified, evidence now suggests that physical differences are not as prominent as earlier supposed.

What once was considered to be strictly biological is now sometimes interpreted more in cultural terms. One example is that although women are different from men in certain basic needs, they still have the same potential for sexual interest and pleasure. Also what was once considered to be a man's role in sex might now just as readily in some instances be occupied by a woman.

The point is that people need to deal with facts and reality rather than myths and stereotypes. As long as they observe the rules of love and friendship and include spirituality as a part of their marriage, things will usually go the right way.

(11) *Equality*   One of the most important things that a couple can do is to develop the idea of sexual equality. This is one area where it definitely helps to be *think-alikes*. Deciding in advance how important sex is and under what conditions it should take place is always a good idea.

It is particularly important for both marriage partners to assume equal responsibility in promoting an intimate relationship and initiating sexual relations. One way of negotiating this is merely to take turns, one doing it one time and the other the next. In this way a couple reaffirms not only their willingness, but ideally also their interest. But whatever the policy might be, the main idea is to do things equally so that this part of marriage does not become a particular domain of one partner or the other.

(12) *Intimacy*   In today's society, characterized by money, sports, prestige, and countless other things, one of the most meaningful comments that a person can make is, "I love and respect my spouse and enjoy living with him or her in an intimate way." In other words, it is

nothing more than abiding by the biblical injunction to be *one flesh*. At the same time it is the number one way of staying happily married and avoiding separation.

(13) *Separation and Divorce* Over one-half, and possibly two-thirds, of the marriages today end in some type of separation. This does not include the large number of people who are actually separated but still remain together despite personal differences. Obviously, this is an alarming situation and emphasizes the importance of adequately preparing for marriage, in the first place, and then later observing correct rules and principles.

(14) *Passion* Passion, or sexual desire, is a vital aspect of the *one flesh* concept and was meant from the beginning to be a part of marriage. Without it there would not be the close union that was intended for a husband and wife. God prohibits this type of relationship outside the marriage bond, but inside he permits and encourages it.

Prior to marriage people are told to *bridle their passions*, which is good advice, but following marriage the bridle should generally be put away. It is extremely important that this type of emotion be present. Under most circumstances, there need not be cause for any uncertainty or hesitation, but rather it should be accepted and valued as an important attribute.

(15) *Familiarity* In a healthy marriage, sexuality is a vital source of familiarity. It is the idea of a couple living together not just in love and friendship but in a special kind of trust and intimacy. At one level a spouse is a good friend, but at a much higher one he or she is literally what the Bible says when it talks about being *one flesh*.

As long as a marital relationship is what it should be, there is a familiar feeling between two people that goes far beyond that pertaining to father or mother, brother or sister, or any other relative or friend. It is a unique concept of oneness, something difficult to explain which transcends all other relationships. One way of expressing it might be to say that a person's spouse is *one's own self*, someone that he or she feels completely comfortable with and wants to be around.

(16) *Marriage Bonding*   When the *one flesh* concept was first introduced, as recorded in the Bible, it comprised three important purposes. One of these was the perpetuation and strengthening of the marriage bond. The implication at that time, however, was that something more was needed than just the usual qualities of love and friendship, something very different and out of the ordinary.

In essence, it involved an actual bonding between husband and wife which, if properly observed, would promote a successful marriage. Its specific purpose was to cement two people, as it were, and keep them together. Along with spirituality and procreation, it was deemed to be the main thing that was necessary, as long as those participating did their part.

And yet ironically, it is this same idea that is now causing people to separate. What was originally meant to bring them together is instead driving them apart. This is confirmed by marriage counselors everywhere who state that a large percentage of separations and divorce, if not most of them, is definitely the result of problems relating to sexuality.

(17) *Fidelity*   The number one safeguard against infidelity, adultery, and separation is a happy and

successful marriage. As long as couples maintain an appropriate amount of religion in their lives and remain sexually active and compatible, the implied promise exists that they will be more apt to stay together. Consequently, it is vital that they participate in a *one flesh* relationship.

Nowhere is this made more plain than in the seventh chapter of First Corinthians in the Bible. In an epistle to the people of Corinth, the Apostle Paul stated how important it was for couples not only to be faithful to one another but to pay close attention to sexuality in their marriages. He specifically warned them against withholding themselves lest they encourage immorality and marital infidelity.

(18) *Job Descriptions*   A so-called job description of a *wife* technically does not include caring for children, keeping house, washing clothes and cooking meals. Nor does that of a *husband* mean going to work each day, providing for his family, or doing yard work. These activities pertain mainly to brotherly love and friendship and are engaged in by couples for the mutual benefit of one another.

The real essence of a husband and wife is much more narrow and limited. It is nothing more than the *one flesh* principle mentioned in the Bible. Whereas one situation is strictly platonic, such as might exist between two good friends or a brother and sister, the other is characteristically sexual as well as friendly.

As a consequence, the condition that sets marriage apart from all other social relationships is the concept of husband and wife. It is the only type of union requiring a legal ceremony as far as religion and morality are concerned. On the other hand, as long as there are no sexual relations involved, a couple could live together unmarried indefinitely. The latter might not always present a good appearance socially, but in a technical way, there would be nothing wrong with it.

(19) *Husband and Wife* It is easy for a woman to stop being a wife, and in the case of a man the same for a husband. They might continue being a good father and mother, grandparents, or whatever, but in their unique role as a couple, the situation can easily change. Anytime that one or the other gets involved in outside activities to the extent that intimacy is lacking or no longer exists, it is evident that a marriage is degenerating or has come to an end, even though the couple is still living together.

This makes it important from the outset for married people to prioritize their relationships. Husband and wife come first, in other words, and after that the children, father and mother, friends and associates, or whatever the order might be. But the vital thing, according to the way it is established in the Bible, is for the marital union to be number one, and this definitely includes maintaining an active sexual relationship.

(20) *Culture and Biology* Despite so-called gender differences which have often been publicized in regard to sexuality, at least some of them now appear to be giving way to more accurate information. Examples of this are that men and women potentially have similar capacities for sexual pleasure and also that some of the alleged differences between them are culturally imposed rather than biologically inherited.

It is reasonable to say that God never really intended for a *one flesh* relationship to inflict upon couples some of the differences which have been suggested. Such a thing contradicts logic as well as reason. But if and when they do occur, they might well be the result of culture instead of biology. The divine plan is more likely to be one where husband and wife participate in sex equally, each sharing the responsibility of initiating relations and also encouraging intimacy.

(21) *New Focus on Sexuality* When it seems that biological differences are affecting a sexual relationship, such as slow arousal or a low sex drive, it might be that all that is needed is for a marriage partner to do what is necessary to become more interested. In spite of the special attraction that sex is supposed to have, people still need to nurture it sometimes and find a more important place for it in their lives. Traditionally, it is more often the wife who allegedly has this kind of problem. Yet once again she might be affected by cultural and personal circumstances rather than those which are mainly biological, and the solution again comes down to thinking more about one's spouse and the sexual part of marriage.

(22) *Knowledge and Skills* One of the most important things for any married couple to accomplish is to acquire the basic knowledge and skills pertaining to sexuality, using them for the purposes of procreation, marital bonding, and spirituality. Few aspects are more vital in a marital relationship, and as such they become a thing of beauty as well as utility. It sometimes requires dedication and hard work to achieve them, but the resulting rewards are usually worth the effort, including a happy and lasting marriage.

(23) *Spouse Abuse* The biblical injunction pertaining to marriage definitely implies that a husband and wife should be involved mutually in a sexual way. Reasons for this are many, one of them being both physical and mental health. In psychological ways especially, it is important for both partners to participate in marital sex, and when one or the other decides that it should

come to an end, it not only weakens a relationship but can also result in serious spouse abuse. Obviously this is a condition that should not be inflicted upon any married couple.

The anxiety and frustration that arises from such abuse, although much less publicized, not only affects romance and intimacy but extends into other areas as well, including spirituality, jobs and occupation, inter-family relationships, and the ability to cope with many different kinds of life situations.

(24) *Definition of Marriage*   From a religious and moral point of view, a *husband* is someone who can provide for his wife in a manner that no one else can. And the same is true for a *wife*. She is the only one who can benefit her husband in ways that are morally impossible for any other person.

What this means is that almost all of life's needs can be furnished by a large variety of people, including friends, relatives, doctors and ministers, but in the very limited things pertaining to an intimate and moral rela-tionship, there is only one person to whom a woman can go, and the same applies to a man. It is the single aspect of marriage and morality that is always explicit and defin-itive.

An important definition of the word *marry*, in fact, is *to unite intimately*, which suggests that even though a legal ceremony has been performed, an actual union or marriage does not occur until a couple joins together as *one flesh*. It is at this point that a marital union is consummated. Previously there was a type of partnership but technically no marriage.

(25) *Important Questionnaire*   Before a marriage ever takes place, it might be well for a couple to submit to

a certain set of questions given by a marriage counselor, ecclesiastical authority, or some other such person. The questions could include the following:

1. Are you willing and prepared to enter a permanent sexual relationship?

2. Will you promote this type of union as well as endorse it?

3. Do you feel that you definitely know what you are getting into and also what is expected of you?

4. Do you realize that sexual relations are not an optional part of marriage as long as both partners want them to continue?

5. Are there any problems which you have that might interfere with such a relationship?

Such are the twenty-five comments and suggestions, therefore, which might help a couple prepare for marriage and significantly strengthen the bond between them. Certainly they are not meant to be a comprehensive list, nor are they intended to be a remedy for all marital problems, but especially as far as the latter is concerned, they can do much to correct or prevent them. And in the process, some of the figures represented in the merging circles theory might well begin to merge more completely, whereas otherwise they could spread even farther apart.

(a)

(b)

(c)

But whatever the circumstances, the main thing is for the ingredients of friendship and sexuality to be in the section where the circles merge. Especially when the amount of merging is small, it is important that these two qualities be present.

In addition, it is good to remember how this part of marriage originated and also who the author is. There is no doubt but what God himself is the one who devised the plan for sexual relations and caused it to be put into practice. He is the main one who endorses it. As a consequence, the plan is almost always obligatory as far as marriage is concerned, and unless a person understands this and agrees with the terms involved, he or she probably should not get married.

Also marriage is much more likely to be successful if people are in good health sexually, as well as physically, spiritually, and emotionally. When all of these aspects are brought together in the right combination, marital success is more apt to occur.

It is vital, however, that both husband and wife stay sexually active, appreciating the ability and gift that have been given to them and resisting any inclination to discontinue a *one flesh* relationship. Moreover, the idea of equality in promoting intimacy should be carefully observed, each partner taking the initiative. Although the latter might seem more difficult for a woman sometimes because of cultural or biological influences, it is nevertheless the kind of undertaking where she has the responsibility as much as a man.

Unfortunately, women have been conditioned down through the years, and not just years but centuries, to be less dominant and aggressive, including a reticence pertaining to sex. Too often they have been the object of intimidation and abuse, and for whatever reasons have been suppressed and kept in the background. In various parts of the world it is still this way.

But during the last century especially, the situation has taken a turn, and at present women continue to acquire an equal status with men, both politically and economically. In many ways it is obvious that they have reversed things in a new direction. And while this is true, it brings up a very interesting observation. Just as women have overcome suppression in such areas as politics and the work field, the same is now taking place in regard to intimacy and some of the more personal aspects of marriage.

In the opinion of one authority, women are now giving expression to that which has long been imprisoned within them, the reality being that not only are they acquiring sexual equality with men, but in regard to intimate pleasure, they are actually capable of larger amounts of it and for a longer period of time. The potential is definitely there, in other words, and for many women it is just a matter of taking the initiative and assuming a different kind of role.

Again the important thing is for couples to join together and do things the right way, which in this case is simply the way advocated in the Bible. In no other place is there more dependable information. The promise still exists that if a husband and wife will cleave to one another and be one flesh, they will have a much better chance for a successful relationship.

And probably the best method of accomplishing this is to be knowledgeable and informed from the very beginning. People should use the time of courtship not just as an opportunity to become better acquainted but to learn more about the different aspects of marriage including those pertaining to sex. Although the latter is a topic they too often might inadequately discuss, it is imperative in appropriate situations that they do so.

It is also important to get good counseling. To read one or more books on sexual relations, for example, written by someone regarded as competent and professional, can be an invaluable investment. This is particularly true when the counsel includes a religious point of view along with the secular. The right kind of author can provide a comprehensive discussion of marriage as well as give specific knowledge and information pertaining to intimacy.

And finally, the most significant thing that might be said about marriage is that it should be enjoyable! Along with its many other aspects and qualities, it ought be interesting and pleasurable. This is one of the benefits of a couple cleaving together and being one flesh, and it was an important reason for implementing such a concept in the first place.

Sexual relations especially were intended to be a source of enjoyment. They were to be the means of drawing couples together, not only for the purpose of having a family but to ensure the stability and perpetuation of marriage itself. The object was to provide an incentive for togetherness, a type of mystery and intrigue that would be appealing to people and help them build a marital relationship.

An important part of this, however, was that there was also the spiritual connection. Beginning with the honeymoon, the coming together of husband and wife was to be a type of religious rite and ceremony, one in which to renew a covenant and celebrate the important event of marriage. It was to be a reunion that would take place often, rather than occasionally, so that the marital bond could be continually reinforced and strengthened.

All of this again suggests the importance of the honeymoon itself and the idea of viewing that event as a standard. It is remembering how marriage life was in the beginning, especially in regard to intimacy, and also how it can continue in the present and into the future. It encourages couples to pay attention to those things which are particularly important, including cleanliness and personal appearance, just as they did while courting, and also staying interested in the feelings of romance such as *curiosity, fascination,* and *imagination.* In short, it is doing whatever is necessary to keep things as they used to be and not let intervening distractions take their place.

And although this kind of thinking might be regarded as idealistic by some, and perhaps even naive by others, still it is logical reasoning and sound advice. Indeed it is the same kind of principle that can be applied to rekindling an interest in sexuality if and when it begins to decline. Recalling pleasurable experiences pertaining to sex and focusing on them can again make this part of marriage more interesting and worthwhile. It is simply a matter of conditioning, substituting one type of thinking in place of another.

The significant thing, whether it be one marriage partner or both, is to give the subject of sex the status and importance it deserves. Again it is a matter of *doing* things the correct way, paying one's *do's,* as it were, in order to obtain the right kind of relationship and preserve a marriage. Certainly it is the logical way of making marital living more feasible and interesting, and at the same time much less complicated. Briefly stated, it is the biblical way and the Lord's way.

The idea is also a very explicit one. Make sexuality

an important part of marriage, observing it spiritually as well as physically, and the result will be *closeness* and *familiarity*. Avoid it or take it away, and there will be feelings of *distance* and *separation*. The quickest way for a couple to become strangers, in other words, is to ignore the counsel of cleaving together and being one flesh. There are other ways it can happen, but this is the main one.

So as things turn out, the teacher and student in the marriage class that day were definitely right. Marriage *can* be a very complicated thing sometimes and should never be taken lightly. Nor should it be entrusted to those who are unknowledgeable and unprepared for it. Yet what they did not say on that occasion is that there is also a positive view along with the negative. Even though separation and divorce are rapidly increasing, there is still a very meaningful way to marital success, and it is nothing more than that which is found in the second chapter of Genesis in the Bible.

Moreover, what makes this idea even more important is that it is not only effective and reliable but pleasurable and enjoyable as well. And for most people in the world today, there is no better offer than that!

Epilogue

Everyone deserves a happy marriage! Certainly it is something that was intended from the beginning. Yet it is like a lot of other things. One has to earn it by obeying the rules.

And although the rules might be many, the most important by far is the one found in the Bible which says that a couple should cleave to one another and be *one flesh*. It is the thing that gets marriage off to a good start, and it is the same thing which can keep it going.

If years pass and both marriage partners decide to discontinue such an arrangement, it might be all right as long as it is mutually agreeable. The important thing is to maintain a happy marriage. But as marriages go nowadays, it might not be worth taking a chance. The safe thing is to obey the rules.

The admonition in the Bible is still loud and clear. It is extremely important for a person, upon reaching the right age, to leave his or her parents and join with a companion of the opposite gender. Prior to that time there is to be no premarital sex. But following a legal ceremony, a sexually-oriented relationship is both authorized and encouraged. And if this kind of union is continued throughout much of a lifetime, supplemented by the qualities of love and friendship, the implied promise is that there will be a happy marriage.

Yet certain rules still have to be followed. A man, for example, needs to be sensitive to his wife's feelings, as well as patient, when she appears to be less inclined toward sexual relations. She might not be disinterested necessarily, but just slower to be aroused. Or it could be that she is on a different timetable. Whatever the situation might be, the husband is the one to help his wife experience at least the same quality of sexuality that he does.

On the other hand, the wife also has her responsibilities, such as not being too coy or modest, or being afraid to show passion. Within the bond of marriage, she should feel free to relax and relate to her husband. Usually there is no legitimate reason, religious or otherwise, why there should be any reservation, although because of cultural circumstances and biological makeup, along with the many domestic things she has to do, she might need to spend additional time in staying sexually active. But the responsibility is still there.

For both marriage partners, in fact, being active in this particular way often requires attention. Yet over a period of time, it can provide many benefits, including increased fitness and vitality and also a youthful disposition. The principle of sex, in other words, can definitely exert a strong and significant influence.

Many people after marriage allow themselves to become unkempt, overweight, and misshapen, but with the right kind of effort and a meaningful emphasis upon sex, they can avoid this. Despite years of change, remaining sexually healthy can prove to be an extremely important incentive to both husband and wife. As one woman author put it, based on things she had seen and read, those who keep themselves healthy in a sexual way not only stay more attractive physically but at the same time add years to their lifetime.

In any case, most people can be confident and optimistic concerning the future of their marriage as long as they obey *the rules*. Especially in a sexual relationship there should be no serious problems, provided they commit to the idea of being *one flesh* and also pledge marital allegiance to their spouses, giving affection and pleasure as well as receiving it.

Any fears, anxieties, or hesitancies pertaining to appropriate sex, particularly as they might be expressed by women, ought to be set aside. Every confidence should be placed in the idea of an intimate relationship. After all, such a thing is specifically heaven's idea, and the Lord himself stands behind it. It is at the very center of his plan for promoting families and strengthening the marital union, as well as developing spirituality.

Definitely it might be said that this one idea, second to very few others, is indispensable in regard to marriage. It is its very being and essence. Although it is something that can undermine a relationship and destroy it if not handled correctly, in the opposite direction it can also nurture it and protect it. In very few instances is any concept more basic or important.

In today's modern society, where marriages and families are both so much in jeopardy, where people are marrying and giving in marriage but not profiting from it, the brief admonition in the Bible pertaining to cleaving together and being *one flesh* might still be the one last hope for marital success and happiness!

What really needs to be said, in fact, might well be expressed in a single paragraph, one found hidden away one day in a file cabinet. No source or publication date is mentioned, and the author is unknown, but the information given constitutes an apt summary of all that has here been written.

"God gave to each man and woman powerful emotions," the paragraph says, "that would attract them to one another and keep them together. Such love must be nourished and kept fresh and vibrant. It is strong so there can be a multiplying and filling of the earth with new life. But it is also given to keep husbands and wives together so they can fulfill each other's needs and prevent the eye of love from straying to others."

Certainly, as to content, these few ideas by themselves communicate an important message to all of those who are married or who plan to be. They state exactly the kind of knowledge and information that couples need to know. Above everything else they are expressions of truth and beauty, and as stated by the English poet so many years ago, they are also the type of things that are most important to us, which is *all that we really know on earth and all that we need to know*!

Note

From a religious standpoint, marriage and family are definitely among the things of greatest importance. But if the marital relationship degenerates because of problems pertaining to sexual intimacy, all of this can go for naught. Indeed it has been said that the way to the kingdom of heaven leads not only through our private living rooms but also through our bedrooms.

The preceding articles were written from this point of view. Hopefully they will provide useful information. Their purpose has always been to suggest that truth is not just a thing of beauty, but also that truth in this particular area is what can help make us free. (John 8:32)

POETRY

By

Clay McConkie

Capri

We stayed the night
At a small hotel
There on the Isle of Capri.

It was just two people
In a room by ourselves
Encircled about by the sea.

The next day
We walked by the cliffs
With no certain place to go.

Mount Vesuvius
Was in the distance
And the blue Mediterranean below.

I remember that day
And how free we were,
Alone just the two of us,

Until toward evening
When we hurried back
To get on board the bus.

From then until now
There have been carefree times,

At least there have been for me,

But nothing to compare
With those quiet hours
We spent on the Isle of Capri.

Woman at a Grocery Store

I saw a woman
coming out of a store
carrying groceries in her arms,
someone in a hurry
to get home
to prepare a meal
for her family.

And I thought to myself,
I hope you're happy,
Mrs. Jones or Mrs. Smith,
or whoever you might be.
I hope you go home each day
to a kind husband,
one who provides you
with a good living,

Who is not too occupied
with his work or his friends,
and not too ambitious
except for paying attention to you,
loving you, and trying
to make you happy.

I also wondered
at the time
what her own personality
was like,
how well adjusted
she was,
or maybe how complicated,
and how she woke up
to the world each day

and coped with everyday living.

As though I were
some kind of personal guardian,
or minister or priest,
I took the liberty that day
of silently pronouncing upon her
a blessing,
one that told her to be happy
and enjoy simple pleasures,
also to shun boredom
and not to expect too much
out of life.

But most of all, I told her
to be faithful to her marriage,
to be spiritual and modest,
a true handmaid of the Lord,
yet not afraid
to share one spirit and one flesh
with her husband,
to show love and passion and respect.

As she put her groceries
in the car
and finally drove off
that day,
I feared for her,
seeing how pretty she was
and how confident,
and knowing
how marriages often fare.

Yet who knows, I thought.
Maybe she is one of the chosen ones,

one of the designated ones,
one of those
who will be happy,
after all,
and make it through,
despite everything possible
that might happen.

A Simple Thing

It's such a simple thing
To walk across the lawn
Among the pines and trees,

To stop and talk
And spend the afternoon,
Doing what you please.

We could have done it many times,
The two of us,
But we didn't,
And I wish we had.

I wish we had taken the time more often
To walk in the park,
To enjoy each other's company
And perhaps remark

What a nice day it was.
We had the time.
We weren't that busy.
It's too bad.

We should have stopped and said hello
All over again,
Renewed one another's acquaintance,
And then laughed

To think we had done
Such a simple thing.
Why didn't we?

Why did we wait
And think that tomorrow
Would always such pleasures bring?

Why didn't we stop and do it then?
It was such a simple thing.

Equality

In days to come
you will probably say once again
that I should have tried harder
and been more aggressive
and persistent,
that I should have paid more attention
to some of the small things
that would have caused you
to respond.

Maybe I did some of this,
and maybe I didn't.
But it's too bad when anyone
is put in a position
where he or she has to keep asking
or reminding
or always mentioning things.
There is no equality here.

In this situation
one definitely ranks superior
over the other
and usually has the advantage.

While one enjoys the convenience
of waiting for the right time and place,
the other is put on hold
and unnecessarily kept waiting,
sometimes for a week,
or a month,
or even a year.
Again there is no equality here.

It would be much better,
it seems to me,
If each person enjoyed equality.

A Place by the Sea

We knelt at the altar
And prayed that day,
And then I took
My bride away

To a country place
Beside the sea,
A private place
For her and me.

I was hers
And she was mine.
The world was gone,
And so was time.

We walked alone
Along the hill
And picked
The yellow daffodil.

I wished her always
By my side,
My beautiful, happy,
Youthful bride.